Unglued & Tattooed

Unglued & Tattooed

How to Save Your Teen from Raves,
Ritalin, Goth, Body Carving, GHB, Sex,
and 12 Other Emerging Threats

Sara Trollinger

Founder of the House of Hope

with Mike Yorkey

LifeLine
Press

A Regnery Publishing Company • Washington, DC

Library of Congress Cataloging-in-Publication Data

Trollinger, Sara.
    Unglued & tattooed : how to save your teen from raves, ritalin, goth, body carving, GHB, sex, and 12 other emerging threats / Sara Trollinger with Mike Yorkey ; foreword by Mark McCormack.
        p. cm.
    "A guidebook for parents"
    Includes index.
    ISBN 0-89526-169-3
        1. Parent and teenager. 2. Child rearing. 3. Parenting. 4. House of Hope (Orlando, Fla.) I. Title: Unglued and tattooed. II. Yorkey, Mike. III. Title.

HQ796 .T72 2001
649'.125—dc21

                                                                    2001038367

Published in the United States by
LifeLine Press
A Regnery Publishing Company
One Massachusetts Avenue, NW
Washington, DC 20001
www.lifelinepress.com

Distributed to the trade by
National Book Network
4720-A Boston Way
Lanham, MD 20706

Printed on acid-free paper
Manufactured in the United States of America

10 9 8 7 6 5 4 3 2

BOOK DESIGN BY JULIE LAPPEN
SET IN JANSON

Books are available in quantity for promotional or premium use. Write to Director of Special Sales, Regnery Publishing, Inc., One Massachusetts Avenue, NW, Washington, DC 20001, for information on discounts and terms or call (202) 216-0600.

Scripture in Chapter 15 taken from the HOLY BIBLE, NEW INTERNATIONAL VER-SION ®. NIV®. COPYRIGHT © 1973, 1978, 1984 by International Bible Society. Used by permission. All rights reserved.

Grateful acknowledgment to Focus on the Family for permission to reprint quotation from A. C. Green (Chapter 9) and Ted Bundy interview excerpt (Chapter 13).

Contents

Foreword

THE TRIPOD-MOUNTED CAMERA WAS IN PLACE, and I was led to a director's chair on the grounds of the House of Hope.

I had agreed to give an on-camera "sound bite" that the House of Hope could use in a promotional video about this fantastic home for troubled teens. When the cameraman motioned that he was ready, the director yelled, "Action!"

I knew what I wanted to say, so I said it.

"In this world, there are millions of people that have vision and have dreams," I began. "There are thousands of people that try to bring these visions and dreams to a place where they can execute them. And there are hundreds of people that execute their visions and dreams, but occasionally you find someone who executes a dream and reaches to the heavens. Such a person is Sara Trollinger, and such a place is the House of Hope."

I meant every word. Sara and her staff have changed hundreds of teen lives—for the better—since 1985. I know because I have witnessed the results firsthand: my wife, Betsy, and I became involved with the House of Hope a number of years ago.

The House of Hope has an astonishing 95 percent success rate of restoring rebellious, drug-ridden, cult-involved, sexually abused, and hurting teenagers back to their families—a statistic that is almost unbelievable in this day and age. Being able to help with the problems of today's teenagers has been a gratifying experience for Betsy and me. One way we've been able to participate has been a simple act: every few weeks, we invite all the boys and girls from the House of Hope over to our Orlando home for the day.

We are fortunate to live on Lake Chase and to have a nice-sized pool and spa in our back yard. We let the kids water-ski and wake-board on the lake, frolic in our pool, hit tennis balls on our tennis court—and then let them eat us out of house and home. We love hosting these teenagers, but you can always tell when any of the kids are new to the program. They are sullen, overly rambunctious, and often disrespectful to the staff members. They have "issues" they're still working on.

When I see them a few months later, the changes are dramatic. "Hi, Mr. McCormack," they'll say, as they look me in the eye and shake my hand. "Thanks for inviting us over today." *Their attitudes are respectful.* There is something about them that wasn't there before. They have *changed.* They respect those in authority, play by the rules, and respond to direction. They are not perfect by any stretch of the imagination, but they've come a long way in the right direction.

That's why you're going to enjoy this book. Sara Trollinger and those assisting her at the House of Hope are going to help you navigate the turbulent teen years—the period when adolescents rock your family boat and threaten to capsize everything you've done to raise them as good kids. The teen years come upon families like a sudden squall, but with a lot of love and attention, firm and consistent discipline, and tons of relationship-building moments, you and your teens can survive the storms.

Mike Yorkey has told this incredible story in a way that will give hope to parents of troubled teens. You will learn more about why the House of Hope is special and why this home for troubled teens has been replicated in twenty-seven cities across the nation. You will be introduced to one of the world's extraordinary women, Sara Trollinger, whose vision and determination made this whole thing possible.

That's why I heartily recommend *Unglued & Tattooed*. If you will invest the time it takes to read this book, you will be given the tools to execute *your* vision and dreams for your children, just as Sara has executed her dream at the House of Hope.

MARK McCORMACK
CEO of International Management Group

Introduction

IT HAPPENS QUICKLY, doesn't it?

Children grow up rapidly, shedding their youth-choir countenance for a fire-breathing demeanor—known as "adolescence"—seemingly overnight. They challenge you at every turn and seek their peers' advice for everything from what clothes to wear to finding "protection" for their Friday night dates.

What happened to my little girl? you ask.

She's still your little girl. It's just that she's experiencing a typical transition from childhood to adolescence. The final third of your parenting years is the most crucial stage. Lose them now, and you could lose them forever.

It's not my intention to scare you. I prefer to see the teen years in a positive light because these can be the best years of your lives together. It's exciting to watch our offspring mature into young adults, full of hope and vim for a future that looks boundless to them. The fact that you are holding this book in your hands tells me that you are vitally interested in your children's welfare and future. I'm afraid that too many parents of adolescents these days are AWOL—absent without leave. They've abdicated their parental role to busyness, indifference, laziness, or a lack of desire—or ability—to engage their teens. A smaller percentage of fathers and mothers (especially single parents) is afraid to step in and offer parental leadership, either because they have no idea what to do or because they lost the upper hand long ago with their children. Some fear their children are already delinquents or are headed for serious problems.

Maybe your teens aren't that bad off. Maybe they're just a little rebellious. Maybe they've gotten into a little bit of trouble with the law for shoplifting or drinking underage at a party. Maybe they're doing what you did as a teen. But you want something better for them. You want them to go through life without experiencing the pain and rejection you felt. You want to protect them from a world that does not have their best interests at heart or that seeks to exploit them.

Maybe you haven't lost the upper hand, but your "grip" on your teens is tenuous at best. If so, and your desire is to learn what makes teens tick, what challenges lie before them today, and how you can mold their behavior without losing them from your team, then you've come to the right place.

You'll lose your teens if you don't know their world. Unless you're aware of what's on their radar screens, you will not be able to "relate" to them and their world. Unless you know about all the media coming at them (Hollywood films, TV shows, music, Instant Chat, MP3s), you will not know what's being whispered into their ears. This doesn't mean you have to watch every teen-targeted movie, buy the latest Puffy Combs CD, spike your hair, or wear short skirts—teens hate parents who adopt their fashions. But you do need to understand where they are coming from. This book will help you do that.

My Background

You may wonder why I've "won the right to be heard," a commonly invoked phrase in today's language. Well, let me tell you a little about my background. I've been interested in young people ever since I graduated from the University of North Carolina in the mid-1950s with a bachelor's degree in education. I couldn't wait to get into the classroom, so I began teaching right away. After teaching in North Carolina public elementary schools for five years, I moved to Florida and taught in the Orange County school system while I pursued a master's degree in exceptional education from the University of South Florida in Tampa. Earning this master's in 1967 allowed me to start working with emotionally handicapped students at junior high schools. I also taught behind bars in the Orange County Juvenile Detention Center.

I became part of the social service "system," and one thing I learned is that the system was a revolving door for these teenagers. In they came, and out they went. Two weeks later, in they came again, only to be released again a few days later. When I mentioned to my colleagues that these teens were coming and going without receiving any lasting help, I received a collective shrug.

"There's nothing you can do about it," said one.

"Don't worry. Just do what you can," counseled another.

One thing I have learned over the years is that hurting adolescents are usually unable to respond properly to authority figures or relate constructively to their peers. To counteract those challenges, they need to live in a loving, stable family-like environment—such as a group residential home where the teenage residents can learn to accept responsibility, submit to authority, and get along with peers and adults. In such a setting, they can also receive help for their "issues" through group, family, and individual counseling.

But where would I start? Well, I talked with five friends about my dream of starting a group home for troubled teens. We got together and opened a bank account with $200 in late 1984. Then one day, I happened to call a certain lady to ask if she knew of some property that we could purchase.

This woman said she did have a piece of property with two small buildings on it, but she would be listing it with a real estate agent the following morning. I asked if I could see it, and she gave me the address. That afternoon, when I stepped on that property on 30th Street near downtown Orlando, I knew that's where we were supposed to be.

I inquired about the asking price.

"I'm listing it for $117,000," she said. That sounded like millions to me since we only had $200.

"What do you want it for?" she asked.

I explained my great desire to start a home for troubled teens, and she listened intently.

"Oh, I've always had a heart for teenagers," she said. "I'll tell you what. Let me talk with my husband, and we'll come up with a final figure before we put the property on the market."

When she called back several days later, she said, "If you want the property, you can have it for $95,000."

I didn't hesitate. "We'll take it!" I exclaimed.

"Good. Then I'll need a down payment."

"Will you accept $200?"

"Yes, but you'll have to come up with the rest of the money at closing."

The next day, I received a letter from the Edyth Bush Foundation, a philanthropic organization, regarding a grant request we had made. The letter announced that we had been approved for $95,000. That was a miracle! We walked away from the closing with our original $200 and started the House of Hope.

Several of my friends volunteered to help me fix up the property, which was badly in need of repair. Walls needed to be painted, carpet had to be replaced, windows were washed, and the grounds were spruced up in anticipation of the arrival of our first three girls. Finances were so tight that first year we held garage sales and put on fundraising spaghetti dinners to buy groceries and pay the bills.

One day I was invited to appear on a local TV show, and after the taping, I bumped into Charley Reese, an *Orlando Sentinel* syndicated newspaper columnist. He had heard me talking about the House of Hope, which intrigued him. Charley listened while I described some of the wondrous things happening at 1010 30th Street.

"Not only am I touched by what you're doing, but I applaud your desire to do it without government funds," he told me. "Would it be okay if I wrote a story about the House of Hope?"

Would it be okay?

The following Monday, Charley's inspiring article about the House of Hope hit the streets. That same morning, President Ronald Reagan flew to Central Florida from Washington, D.C., to dedicate the new Epcot Center at Disney World.

After the ceremony, President Reagan boarded Air Force One for the return trip to Andrews Air Force Base. During his flight, an aide handed the president a copy of the *Orlando Sentinel*, among other things, to read. He turned to the *Sentinel*'s editorial page where he happened to come across Charley's column about the lives being changed at the new House of Hope.

Charley Reese's eloquent words must have touched President Reagan's heart. Why else would the president reach into his briefcase, pull out his checkbook, and pen a $1,000 check to the House of Hope from his personal account? Why else would he compose a nice note and ask an aide to mail it?

This began a relationship between the House of Hope and the Reagans that continues to this day. The highlight of our relationship culminated in 1990 when former president Reagan visited the House of Hope with his wife, Nancy, shaking hands with each of our nineteen girls and taking a tour of the facilities. When one of our girls asked Mr. Reagan why he was so interested in them, he replied that he had fallen in love with the work of the House of Hope after reading that newspaper article back in 1985.

Mr. Reagan is just one of hundreds of persons who have assisted our nonprofit organization, financially supporting us or volunteering their time to scrub floors, hang wallpaper, sew clothes, wash dishes, mow lawns, and cook meals. More importantly, I've had the wonderful privilege of working with dozens of others to care for, counsel, and rehabilitate hundreds of teenage boys and girls since 1985.

We take in teens who have suffered terrible physical and emotional abuse from the mothers and fathers who brought them into this world. We take in teens who can't remember the last time they got through the day without getting high from drugs or alcohol. We take in teens who are just one wrong step away from a prison term. We take in teen girls who have been "date raped" or have been the objects of sexual gratification from parents or stepparents. We take in teens who have rejected authority figures. We take in teens whose greatest desire is to end their suffering by taking their own lives. In short, we take in what society calls "throwaways."

We've helped turn around the lives of these teen boys and girls who stay with us for an average of eight to eighteen months, depending upon the seriousness of their "issues." Through education and spiritual guidance, administered in a loving, home-style environment, efforts are made to heal the hurts of the children, as well as those of their families. That's why we've also counseled hundreds of parents over the years and successfully put them back together with their children, since family reconciliation is our ultimate goal. We are proud of our 95 percent success rate in restoring teens to their families.

Many reporters, attorneys, judges, counselors, and interested parents have dropped by the House of Hope over the years to find out how we've done it. Having learned a few things about raising teens over the years, we are happy to share our advice throughout this book. But at the same time, please know that we don't have all the answers—just a lot of love and experience.

The road to being a great parent of teens is paved with two things: communication and relationship. If I received a $20 bill for every time a teen said to me, "Miss Sara, if my parents would have just communicated with me instead of getting angry all the time, I wouldn't have gotten so messed up," our fundraising efforts would be over. To help you communicate better with your teens, I've included "Discussion Starter" questions following each chapter that you can use to get the verbal ball rolling with your teens. The key, after asking these questions, is to listen to their responses. What they say should prompt many interesting follow-up discussions. The talks you have with your teens should be the best part of this book.

I've seen clinical reports showing that kids who get into self-destructive behavior are kids who grew up spending very little time communicating with their parents. Remember when your children were in their preschool years and they soaked up—and repeated—everything you said? Remember how they asked you every question they could think of, including some real beauties like "Do worms yawn?" "Where do birds spend the night?" and "Can Barney see me?" Those questions were priceless, as was your interaction.

Regular, matter-of-fact conversations between a parent and child are the foundation of learning right and wrong. Put another way, conversations and relationships between parents and children are the main conduits for establishing morality. We will be emphasizing this theme throughout the book, and we will give you the tools to talk with your teens.

For reasons of privacy we have changed the names of the teens quoted in this book. But their stories are real, their insights are illuminating, and through them you can learn how to protect and guide your children through their turbulent teens.

Nothing to Rave About

IF YOU LOG ON TO AMERICA ONLINE and inquire about the hottest nightclubs in the country, you will discover that the Firestone Club in Orlando tops the list. Sure, you can find bigger or more famous nightclubs in New York City, but for square foot per square foot of dance parquet, AOL partygoers rank Firestone Club as the best "dance club" in the United States.

Perhaps the Firestone Club's lofty status can be attributed to Orlando's position as the international party crossroads of the world. There's no doubt that our year-round warm weather and proximity to Disney World, Epcot Center, Universal Studios, Sea World, and other resorts lure millions to Central Florida every year. Many of those are teenagers who step off the widebodies at Orlando International Airport in a party mood.

Clubs like the Firestone know how to pack them in, and they do so by creating an otherworldly atmosphere that begins with brilliant and mood-altering lighting and is underscored by pulsating, frenetic music. These nightclubs also turn a blind eye to underage drinking, drug taking, and sex in the bathrooms. Technically speaking, you have to be eighteen years old to enter, but the beefy bouncers operate under a no-questions-asked policy. Even if they "card" a gum-smacking, pimply teen who looks as though she still belongs in middle school, the bouncers will accept the flimsiest of fake IDs, as long as her money is green.

> I've seen kids twelve, thirteen years old at raves. Nobody got ID'd; all they wanted was your money. People sold pills, cocaine, and ecstasy—a drug that took a while to hit you, but once it did, you'd start dancing crazy and doing weird stuff.
>
> —*Jimmy*, age sixteen

The moneymaking success of "legit" clubs like the Firestone has created a market for dance clubs flying underneath the radarscope of many parents of teenagers. They are called "raves," and these midnight-to-dawn dance debauches have spawned a new hedonistic subculture. The rave scene is mainly a major metropolitan phenomenon, but they are catching on in Middle America, where the "clubbing" mentality remains a novelty. There is something about the marriage of modern electronic music and the rave culture's celebration of childlike escapism through dancing and drug taking that makes raves something to watch for in the next few years.

Teens would tell you that raves are just another dance party for kids, but, in reality, raves have a unique ability to create an anything-goes atmosphere in which teens drink till they pass out, ingest mind-altering drugs by the handful, and (for the males) enjoy indiscriminate sex with girls too stoned to remember where or who they are.

You say you haven't heard about raves? That's because these energetic all-night happenings are staged in the wee hours of the night in clandestine areas, usually a rusty-roofed warehouse rented for the evening by a here-today, gone-tomorrow "promoter." The venue is transformed into Party Central by a crew that installs colorful lights, computerized lasers, blinking strobes, a hefty sound system, and stands that sell alcohol. The promoters also hire jive-talking DJs proficient at getting a dance floor moving by playing songs such as "Ecstasy" (an anthem to drug taking), "Rough Sex," and "I Do Both Jay and James" (the latter song being an exhortation to "get it on").

The dimly lighted floor is transformed into a sweaty soup of hopped-up kids. They dance with wiry abandon, gyrating faster and faster with the beat. "Break dancing," in which teens jump up and down on the floor, performing tricks and spins, is still popular these days. The newest thing is "liquid dancing" in which the boys and girls pretend they have a ball between them, which they "form" with their hands. This dance is very seductive and suggestive of sex.

If you look closely, you'll see teen boys and girls mimicking other sexual practices. There's a girl on her knees while her date sidles up to her and pretends to receive oral sex. Another girl presents her blue-jeaned backside to her partner, who pretends to "mount" her. Other couples dance as close as they can to each other, then begin dipping up and down in synchronization. Looks like sex standing up to me. This dance form is known as "freaking," and it is banned at high schools across the country for obvious reasons. But at rave clubs,

where no chaperones are present, freaking is just the warm-up
before some type of sexual release occurs later that evening.

Packing 'Em In

To fill their warehouse—and their wallets—the promoters get
the word out by "papering" area high schools, independent
record stores, alternative clothing stores, coffee shops, dance
clubs, and local universities with eye-catching flyers advertising
the event. The promoters also build Internet mailing lists since
they know computer-savvy teens can easily find rave Web sites.
They call their raves "Pandemonium" or "Zin Festival," and
they tout themes of brotherly love, peace, and becoming one.

The promoters hide their identities behind bogus companies such as "Mid-Atlantic Productions" or the "Hindenburg
Express." It doesn't matter to the kids *who's* putting on the
rave—they're just interested in partying until their bodies give
out. The promoters, who know that they operate on the out-
skirts of the law, cover their bases by having a backup warehouse ready to go in case the cops shut things down early in
the evening.

Early is a relative term. Most raves advertise a start time
of 10 P.M. or 11 P.M., but no respectable raver would show
up before midnight. Things really start cooking around
1 A.M., and revelers remain at a high-pitched frenzy for many
more hours.

> I can tell you why I went to raves. When I was feeling
> lonely, I felt like I was accepted there. I didn't have to
> worry about anything when I was there. Everything was
> going by so fast.
>
> —*Brittany*, age fifteen

What is a rave? It's kind of like a social function. You see lights, lots of lights, and these glimmering effects while you're on drugs.

—*Kevin*, age seventeen

I loved the rave scene. I would spend from twelve midnight to 3 A.M. getting ready to go out. I put on this clear glow-in-the-dark paint on my face so when I was underneath a black light, my whole face would glow in the dark. The whole rave scene is what you wear. I wore those huge clothes that cost me hundreds of dollars. My pants were so huge and wide-legged that I could barely walk in them. Underneath my pant legs, I hid my drugs. Some clubs did frisk you down, but most didn't.

—*Kayla*, age sixteen

A Short History Lesson

The first raves popped up in the English countryside, outside London and Manchester, back in the late 1980s during the height of Britain's acid-house culture. Early raves were impromptu, secretive events that British teens learned about through word of mouth. It took about five years before raves caught on, on this side of the Atlantic.

Raves have to be seen to be believed, but let me give it a try. Imagine that you're a teenager, riding with your buddies to a Saturday night rave. Six of you have managed to squeeze into a small sedan that comfortably seats four.

Your parents think you're spending the night at a friend's house. Instead, you've been drinking beers and having a good time, waiting until the midnight hour when the *real* party begins. You drive into your city's industrial district, armed with directions. Fortunately, you can hear the rave before you turn on the street where kids are parking cars and walking— well, maybe some of them are stumbling—to the large warehouse seventy-five yards down to the left.

You patiently stand in a long line to enter. As you check out those standing in front of you, you notice that the typical raver wears baggy fatigues, a corporate logo–parody T-shirt, and a backpack. What's in the backpacks? It's not schoolbooks! A better guess would be bottled water and drugs, maybe a few condoms.

The promoters have hired a couple of "security guys" to collect the cover charge and check for IDs, but on this particular evening, "security" is more interested in collecting cash than checking ID cards or backpacks. You hand over a $20 bill and step inside. A kaleidoscope of orange and purple laser lights and dizzying strobes immediately assaults you, all punctuated by the very loud, nonstop beat of electronic dance music called *techno*.

Techno, a distant cousin of disco, contains influences from Kraftwerk, hip-hop, and reggae. The music's purpose is rather simple: get everybody moving to a loud, repetitive, and hypnotic beat so that they can "lose" themselves. The music must take the ravers to another place (wherever that is) while lulling the conscious mind into a stupor. It's time to get your mojo working and suspend yourself in space while you move to the numbing beat. The DJ has an important job at raves, since the success of the events rises and falls on how well he can manipulate the emotions of the revelers swirling to the music.

I think ravers go to the extreme. They really want to walk on the edge of the ledge of a high building. They want to see how far they can take things.

—*Jeremy*, age sixteen

The techno music can be rather hypnotic, but it surely seems to put everyone in a good mood. You can't help noticing that everyone is so *friendly*. Then you remember why everyone is so happy. One of your buddies told you that ravers are big into PLUR, an acronym for Peace, Love, Unity, and Respect. Ravers are caught up in this unity stuff and committed to PLUR. This means they accept everyone who steps inside because raves are a place where you can be what you want to be. Ravers draw kids of all colors, straights, gays, and a few transsexuals, all to one spot. Since ravers construct their own community inside the warehouse walls, anyone who arrives with a good vibe is welcome to be part of the scene.

You continue your tour. Along the walls, you can see groups of three, four of your peers huddling around each other. Upon closer inspection, you notice one of them opening aluminum foil containing cake-like powder. This dealer—the kid next door, actually—is selling hits of heroin, Rohypnol, GHB, and various drugs to bring you down—"landing gear," as he calls it. A few steps away, another guy is handing what looks like a two-liter bottle of water to a friend. Looking around further, you notice something *really* strange: many teens—especially the girls—are walking around with pacifiers in their mouths!

I was only thirteen when I went to my first rave. I had never even done drugs before, except for smoking marijuana a little bit, but I thought these kids were weird. They walked around with glow-in-the-dark baby pacifiers in their mouths. I thought, *What is their problem?* Then I learned that when they were on drugs, usually ecstasy or acid, they would clench their jaws. To protect their teeth, they chewed on pacifiers. These glow-in-the-dark pacifiers and their stringers were pretty funky looking.

—*Sarina*, age sixteen

It's getting darker as you walk farther and farther away from the main staging area. You spot an old couch up against the wall. A teen girl with her dress hiked up to her waist is oblivious as a guy with his pants around his ankles takes advantage of her drug-induced state. Just when you think you've seen enough, you walk into a restroom, where you witness various sex acts being performed, including male on male.

I did have sex a couple of times at the raves. I even saw a couple having sex while they were dancing. Having sex there happened a lot, although the girls wore these tiny little skirts and seemed to ask for it.

—*Alex*, age fifteen

The rave is starting to fill up. Before the evening is over, the warehouse will be packed with a couple of thousand sweaty and stoned kids. Sometimes the party spills out into the neighborhood, where the spaced-out teens score more drugs or find places where they can have sex. They will lose themselves until dawn, which is when the party finally starts to break up. Some are so stoned that they will wake up in places they never thought possible.

As a youth counselor, I've talked to many girls who have gone to raves, and they all told me that they got more than they were bargaining for. Once they entered the rave, they learned that they never had to pay for drugs. This is fairly universal in the teen drug scene. Guys view giving drugs to "chicks" as a down payment for some good times later. At raves, it's not unusual for a girl to be raped three or four times. These sex acts happen in a bathroom stall or out in the open—right in the middle of everything. There is such mass chaos that no one ever knows. Somebody could scream at the top of his lungs, but the music is so loud that no one would ever hear you. The other thing is that these girls are so high that they have very little fight in them. They have been broken down by the rave.

—*Mary*, a House of Hope counselor

The people at the telephone company in downtown Orlando said they were tired of coming to work in the morning and finding naked women lying in their parking lot.

—*Sandy*, a House of Hope counselor

The presence of drugs at raves is universal. Most ravers enter the warehouse expecting to get high, or they feel drugs add to the sensory enhancements of raving. They also believe that drugs can boost their energy for the long night of energetic dancing ahead. Others enjoy the feeling of getting blitzed and escaping whatever their "reality" is. They feel a desire to indulge in the forbidden fruit.

Raves give a false sense of security, a sense that their enclosed environment is a safe place to do drugs. For whatever reason, teens feel tremendous pressure from fellow ravers to let loose and get high on hallucinogenic drugs such as ecstasy. Marijuana is still popular, mainly because of the rave's mellow PLUR mindset. (Remember? Raves are all about peace, love, unity, and respect.) LSD, the cheap psychedelic of the sixties, has made a comeback with the ravers.

Protecting Them from Harm

April, one of our girls at the House of Hope, had a fairly typical experience with raves. "I pretty much started going to clubs and raves when I was in sixth grade," she told me. When I expressed my incredulity that a sixth grader could get past the bouncer, April replied, "You can get a fake ID in a heartbeat if you know the right people. I started off by going clubbing every weekend. I arrived at the Sapphire [a downtown Orlando club] sometime between midnight and 2 A.M. They never really closed until 4 A.M. I just got wasted."

"What was the attraction, April?"

"I think it was just the atmosphere, being with a group of adults," April said. "It was like being free. As long as you were inside the Sapphire, you could get anything. I'd say, 'Hey, give me a shot of vodka,' and they would say, 'Here it is,' and not even check."

"But, April, didn't your parents care where you were?"

"No."

"Well, how did you get out of the house?"

"I said, 'Dad, I'm going to the midnight movie and probably won't be home until three o'clock because we're stopping at Taco Bell to get something to eat.' Stupid stuff like that. On school nights, I'd say I have to go to the library to do some homework and then chill out after the library closes at a friend's house. I thought of them all."

"But what if your dad told you to be back at 10 P.M.?" I asked.

"I'd say, 'Okay, bye, Dad,' and just walk out. Then I'd call at ten o'clock and tell him I was coming home at twelve. See you later."

"But if he said he wanted you home by ten o'clock..."

"Then I'd say, 'See you.' *Click.* And then I'd do what I'd want."

"What would your father do then?"

April thought for a minute. "He would tell me that I couldn't go out with that friend for a week. It really wasn't a big punishment because I would go out with other friends instead."

Now that you have a fairly comprehensive picture of what raves are all about, what can you—the parents of boisterous teens—do to protect your children from harm?

I, along with my counseling staff at the House of Hope, am continually amazed how parents fail to parent, for lack of a more clever word. We call it the "ostrich syndrome," in which the parents turn blind eyes and deaf ears to their teenagers. They put their heads in the sand because they don't want to be involved in their teens' lives or get hassled by being the "bad guy" or "mean mom" if they say no to letting their children go out at night.

Listen to this fairly typical exchange between Jessica, one of our straight-talking House of Hope counselors, and Larry and Sheila, parents of a rebellious fifteen-year-old named Rachel.

Larry: How come I've never heard of raves?

Jessica: Because you're not a teen. You're not in the market. If you went to any area high school and asked what a rave was, you would be blown away that every teen knew the answer, whether they attend them or not.

Sheila: We think Rachel is going to raves. How can we keep her from doing that?

Jessica: First of all, I guess I'd wonder how she could go. Did you allow her to go, or did Rachel just go without your permission?

Larry: She said she was going to a party with some friends. I thought that would be okay, but then another parent told us they were at a rave.

Jessica: Much more is going on here than meets the eye. From a counselor's perspective, if you say to Rachel, "You can't go to the rave," I don't think that you'll get to the issue. I think there's something else going on here, and it's drawing her to the rave.

Larry: You're asking me what's drawing Rachel to these raves? Okay, I give up. What do you think the draw is?

Jessica: The draw is the sex, drugs, and the atmosphere. Rachel wants to be in that atmosphere with thousands of other teens, doing things that appear to be fun.

Sheila: Now that Rachel sneaked out to the rave, we don't know whether we can trust her. What should we do?

Jessica: There's definitely a trust issue going on here. Aside from the fact that she went to the rave, another issue is the friend she's hanging with who took her to the rave. Many kids just don't show up at raves unless they go with friends. Friends are a huge influence. They can be your greatest asset or your worst nightmare, to be honest. Friends make it or break it for teenagers these days because there's so much peer pressure. If they have friends who say, "Come rave with me," and they don't stand up to those friends and say no, they will get sucked in. Initially, they may not be willing to get stoned or have sex, but more than likely they will become involved in those activities. The ravers that I've worked with have told me that raves are an obsession.

Larry: How often do they go during a week?

Jessica: I've worked with teens that have gone three to four times a week; as much as they can do it. More typical is all weekend long—Friday, Saturday, and Sunday. They are just sucked in.

Larry: Since you're saying that it's their friends sucking them in, does that mean I should forbid Rachel from seeing certain friends?

Jessica: That's a catch-22 because when you forbid teens from doing things with the friends they see every day at school, you're going to create a rift with them. My goal as a counselor is to find out what's inside your daughter. What is drawing her to the rave scene? Is she moving toward the rave to feel loved or get attention because she's not getting enough attention from you? What's pulling her there? Is it loneliness, wanting to fit in?

Many troubled teens have identity issues—not knowing where they're accepted. They have a hard time figuring out who they are, so they go out and try this to see whether they fit into these places. Since raves are places where it's pretty easy to be accepted for who you are, you can see what makes it so attractive to needy teens. For those who feel that they can't fit in elsewhere, they can fit there.

Sheila: I'm more pessimistic than Larry. It sounds like it's going to be really hard for us to keep Rachel from going to the rave clubs. Give us some concrete advice. Give me some answers.

Jessica: My question to you, Mom and Dad, is how much time are you spending with Rachel? Larry, are you just coming home from work, eating dinner, and then watching TV the rest of the night?

Larry: I have to put in long hours. I come home around 6:30 from work, and by the time my wife gets food on the table, it's 7:30 or 8:00. Rachel has already eaten something, so she's in her room. She's doing her homework or talking on the phone with some friends.

Jessica: What about weekends?

Larry: You know, when she used to play soccer, I coached the team. Now she doesn't play.

Jessica: Something that I talk to dads about is the importance of establishing a date night with their teen daughters. This is a set time on a set evening when the daughter knows that Dad will spend some time with her doing something. It may sound a little corny, but this has to be something that Dad initiates so that she's not asking for it. That way, the fear of rejection is gone. The last thing she needs to hear is her dad telling her that he doesn't have time for her.

When Dad comes home on date night, it doesn't have to be a huge deal. Make it a special time when she knows she has you to herself. You should be doing something together— eating out, going shopping, taking a drive, going out for a treat, playing tennis, or watching a live sporting event together. The ideas are endless, if you use your imagination.

I believe that dads give something special to their daughters that no one else can give. I believe that dads can give a daughter the feeling that she's beautiful, she's loved, and that she is cherished. Many girls I see have absent fathers, so they're looking to be accepted and loved by the world. If you are taking the time to be with Rachel, she will get something from you, which means she doesn't have to look for love outside the home.

Sheila: What about moms?

Jessica: Moms need to be there so they can be sounding boards for their teens. Teens love to talk if you will give them half a chance. If you work outside the home, I would do everything in my power to be home when the kids come home from school, especially in their teen years.

Teens can get in more trouble between the hours of 3 P.M. to 6 P.M. than almost any other time frame. Do everything you can so the family can eat together. This is a time when you ask how the day went, what's going on. It shows you're being involved.

Another thing I've seen at the House of Hope is that the mood of the house staff—those who live with the boys and girls—affects everyone in the home. We all have bad days. If a father comes home grumbling about his bad day, acts angry, and puts up a wall, he has just created a communication barrier between him and his kids. Be aware of your mood when you come home from work or when your child arrives home from school!

Being a parent these days is much more than providing for physical needs. I have asked girl after girl over the years, including ones with both parents in the home, "Did your dad give you what you needed growing up?"

They say, "Oh, yeah, he gave me an allowance," or "He bought me a used car"—monetary things. Sure, their fathers put food on the table and kept them in clothes, but there wasn't any emotional bonding. I think that's huge.

Larry: Are there certain sports or hobbies mothers and dads can do with their kids?

Jessica: It doesn't matter which sport or hobby a parent enjoys. The important thing is that parent and child pursue an activity *together*. If a father is crazy about NASCAR racing cars but his daughter hasn't the slightest interest in watching a bunch of logoed stock cars go around in 180-mph circles, their relationship will slide off the track. We have tons of kids here at the House of Hope whose dads didn't make an effort to do anything that the kids liked to do. If we turn that scenario around and see the parent pursuing what the child enjoys, then you can have some good results. Sometimes part of being a good parent is putting down your own desires and finding out what your children like to do.

If your daughter likes needlepoint, well, a father doesn't have to sit down and do needlepoint. If he can just show an interest in it—maybe take her shopping for new patterns—then he'll move their relationship forward. A girl told me once that she took up cheerleading because she knew her football-crazy father would watch her cheer from the stands. That's how strongly teens crave attention in parent-child relationships.

Then there are the uninvolved parents. I counseled one girl who loved to play softball. Her dad came to only one game in all the years she played softball—just one game! She loved softball and hoped that he would come to see her play, that this activity would pull her dad into her life. Things didn't work out that way. He wasn't willing to go the extra mile to build a relationship with her.

Let's Do More Than Hope for the Best

Did you catch the gist of Jessica's advice? It boils down to this: Your relationship with your teens is everything. I will be returning to this theme time after time in this book, because what we've found at the House of Hope is that you cannot rebuild teens' lives until you develop a strong relationship with them. The following questions will allow you to gauge the relationship between you and your teens. Take a moment and take your time while you go through them:

◆ Do you take a laissez-faire approach ("kids will be kids") and hope for the best?
◆ Do you think you have a strong relationship with your teens?
◆ What things are you doing together to build your relationship?
◆ Are you involved in their world? Are you looking for things to share with them?

How did you do? Good? Not so good? Now I'm going to introduce the most important part of the book, which will be a series of "Discussion Starter" questions that you will find at the end of every chapter. These questions are designed to peel off a layer or two at a time—much like an onion. They are designed to get you communicating. They are designed to enhance and build your relationships. Be prepared for some exciting, animated—and perhaps even heated—discussions.

Discussion Starter questions can't be asked during moments scheduled in your DayTimer. In other words, writing in "Ask Toby Discussion Starter questions from Chapter 1" for the 2:45 P.M. slot on Saturday afternoon and expecting your teen to be a chatterbox at the appointed hour just won't happen.

I suggest that you take your teens out to a sit-down restaurant or their favorite fast-food outlet with the express desire of talking to them. You can talk while you wash the car together or drive around doing errands—of course, they'll have to turn off their Sony Walkmans, and you'll have to turn off the car radio.

Set some ground rules. Your teens can say anything they want, as long as the remark is respectful. No yelling or name-calling for you or your teen. This is the time for them to begin acting like young adults. Remind your teens that you, as a parent, have set boundaries based on your standards and morality. Here's one way you can say that:

"Sean, I was given a responsibility to raise you and to love you the day you entered this world," you might say. "I'm going to continue to do that, and I'm going to continue being there for you during your adolescent years. You're growing up. I'm excited for you and your future, but I want to help you avoid some of the mistakes that I made and that other teens make."

Discussion Starters

Have you ever heard of rave clubs?
Are there rave clubs in our city (or town)?
Have you ever seen a rave-club flyer?
What goes on at raves?
Do you think you'd ever want to go to a rave?
Have you ever been to a rave?
What was it like?
Did you see anyone OD'ing on drugs?
Do you think raves are a good idea for teens?
What do think about teens going clubbing?
Do they ask for IDs at raves or clubs?

Drugs That Take
You Beyond

THE KIDS AT HOUSE OF HOPE love Detective Scott Perkins. He had been an undercover cop with the Orlando Police Department until he got shot up during a successful hostage rescue a couple of years ago.

I first saw Scott on an Orlando TV program being interviewed about his work. "Parents don't have a clue that their kids are bringing disguised drugs into their homes," said Scott, and I nodded my head in agreement. I knew right away that I had to get in touch with this streetwise cop and bring him to the House of Hope to educate our staff and talk to the teens about the dangers of going back on drugs.

We immediately liked Scott, a friendly, outgoing, and approachable fellow in his mid-thirties. As he regaled us with stories from his undercover days, we soon realized that he is a brave guy who has stayed alive by employing his street-savvy wits. Our kids recognize courage when they see it. I've asked

Scott to be my expert on the teen drug scene because he worked undercover for six years—a long time in that dangerous line of work.

Scott certainly has a way of grabbing the kids' attention. All it takes is for him to start telling a few stories about taking down the bad guys, and our House of Hope kids want to hear more. Throughout much of the 1990s, Scott's job was to infiltrate Orlando's burgeoning rave scene and discover who the drug dealers were. He witnessed their handiwork every weekend at the raves. "I saw it all," he says. "Kids experiencing seizures and blackouts. Kids uncontrollable due to the various 'designer' and 'club' drugs they were ingesting at rave parties. One time I saw a kid shuffle out of the warehouse, drop to the ground, and start flopping like a fish," said Scott. "Then he vomited and spit up foam. It was bad, man."

Scott speaks in a matter-of-fact manner of someone who's seen too many drug overdoses, or "ODs," over the years. He's been in too many Orlando hospital emergency rooms, trying to comfort inconsolable parents who had been asked to identify their dead son or daughter. His earnest prayer—and mine—is that you will never receive that fateful phone call in the middle of the night.

Kids Are Easy Pickings

In the last chapter, I described how raves began as nirvana-like parties in which the zonked-out participants promoted peace, love, unity, and respect. Organized drug dealers have found raves to be easy pickings to sell heroin, GHB, crystal-meth, and other deadly drugs. Remember: the effects of drugs *enhance* the intensity of the music and lights. If someone comes along and says that ecstasy or GHB is the ticket to ride, who's going to say no in such a free-for-all, chaotic atmosphere?

If you are the parent of teenage children, then you are most likely between the ages of thirty-five and fifty-five. Since you came of age in the sixties and seventies—a time when Dr. Timothy Leary was advising everyone to "tune in, turn on, and drop out"—chances are that you experimented with drugs. Maybe you were a consistent user in your teen years. If so, you were part of the first American generation to use such drugs as marijuana and LSD in big numbers. Remember those hazy days? That was an era when drugs swept high school and college campuses and spawned "acid rock" music by the Doors and Steppenwolf. You and your friends argued whether the Beatles song "Lucy in the Sky with Diamonds" was about LSD.

Disco music in the latter half of the 1970s ushered in the next big drug wave—cocaine. Cocaine hydrochloride seemed like the perfect drug for the Studio 54 disco scene. A few years later, drug dealers figured out how to convert coke into crack cocaine, and crack became an epidemic in the 1980s. Law enforcement, community educators, and parents focused on stopping crack in its tracks, giving birth to the "War on Drugs" and First Lady Nancy Reagan's "Just Say No" antidrug campaign.

In many respects, there's nothing new under the sun regarding teenage drug use. What's happening is that kids are being introduced to many different things at a much earlier age than they used to be. In your day, there was a rather orderly progression: teens smoked cigarettes, discovered beer, and moved on to Jack Daniel's. Then they started smoking pot, which was an entryway to acid. For most teens back in the sixties and seventies, this is where their drug use leveled out.

Today's teens still follow the progressive route, although they are prone to skip over several steps. They may start smoking in grade school before ditching the Marlboros for a cigarette with some punch—marijuana. Once that loses its thrill, it's time to experiment with pills such as Valium and Seconol Then their drug use becomes *serious*. They turn their attention to several new "designer" drugs, the most popular being MDMA (methylene dioxymethamphetamine), other-‘ wise known as XTC or "ecstasy." Painted like candy canes or imprinted with Nike swooshes to appeal to adolescents, ecstasy pills are sold on the street for prices ranging from $15 to $25.

"Ecstasy combines the energy that amphetamines give you with the slight hallucinations of LSD," explained Detective Scott. "Plus, ecstasy has components that break down communication barriers, which is why it has been so popular in raves. Ecstasy causes you to ignore the body's warning signals that it needs rest and water. You can literally dance yourself into a heat stroke. If you combine ecstasy with alcohol, which is a diuretic, your body becomes drained of fluids much more quickly. I saw ravers just dance themselves into exhaustion."

Ecstasy comes in various pill forms called "Lightning Bolts," "Doves," "Smurfs," "Bootlegs," "Blue Pandas," and "Pink Triangles." These pills, about the size of aspirin, can be ingested orally, but you don't feel anything for about half an hour. Many kids snort ecstasy in a powder form so they can get high within five to ten minutes.

And what a high. Users experience an abundance of energy and a desire for touching and hugging. Body massages intensify the high, as does sexual behavior. Kids on ecstasy are said to be "rolling," "peaking," "blowing up," or "X-ing." One of the involuntary side effects of ecstasy, however, is teeth grinding and biting the lips and tongue.

Smoking weed and doing acid was boring. I didn't like it. Then one of my friends showed me ecstasy and said I would love it, that it would feel as though my skin was flying off. Ecstasy sounded like fun, so I took it. Most kids have a drug of choice. My drug of choice became ecstasy.
—*Kelli*, age fifteen

I can tell you why kids take more and more drugs. It goes like this: if speed and crack take you up to the fourth floor, then why not go all the way to the twelfth floor and take a chance with harder drugs? Either way, the fall will kill you.
—*Curtis*, age sixteen

Remember that I told you that kids bring their backpacks to rave clubs? I'm going to let Detective Scott tell you what's in the backpack:

When I speak before parents, I pull out a backpack and start taking items out of it. "Everything that is coming out of this pack is drugs or drug paraphernalia," I say. Of course, most parents are thinking about rolling papers, roach clips, and bongs—stuff from the seventies. Not any more these days. The first thing I pull out is an M&M bag. The second thing is a Skittles bag. The next is a Tootsie Roll bag. The fourth is a Blow Pop bag. The fifth is a pacifier. Then I reach down and pull out glow sticks, a Vicks inhaler, a surgical mask, a heavy-duty balloon, a condom, a string, a rubber band, a stick of gum, a Visine bottle, a bottle of water, and a bottle of bubbles. Each one of these items has a very specific function for drug users.

Those using ecstasy suck on a Blow Pop candy or pacifier because the drug makes you grind your teeth and bite your tongue. The M&M and Skittles bags contain ecstasy "rolls" or pills. Kids take a bag of M&Ms, use a knife to cut open a slit, and then dump out the chocolate candies. The candy bag is then refilled with ecstasy pills, which have the same feel as the chocolate candy. They tape up the bag and lay it right on the table in front of everybody's face.

The Tootsie Rolls are the smaller, individually wrapped ones you normally purchase in fifty- or one hundred-packs. The kids go outside and place a few on the sidewalk to let the sun melt them a bit. Then they bring them inside, unwrap them, put an ecstasy tablet inside and rewrap them. The kids do that so they won't get busted. If an undercover cop sees them handing a Tootsie Roll to someone, he probably won't interfere.

The same thing happens with a stick of gum. Dealers unwrap the gum, give it a small hit of acid, and wrap it up again. A kid with a fifty-pack of gum spiked with LSD can walk around school all day with this gum in his backpack. If you asked any cop when the last time was that he searched a piece of gum, he would reply, "Never!"

The Visine bottle, used primarily by sexual predators, is filled with a drug called GHB. They arrive at a rave, notice an attractive girl, strike up a conversation, and when she's not looking, squeeze a couple of drops of GHB into her drink.

GHB works in three stages. In the first stage, she feels sexually aggressive and comes on to a guy. The second stage is when she says she doesn't feel good. The third stage is when she passes out. The guy who doses her knows all the stages. As soon as she complains about not feeling good, he suggests taking her outside for some "fresh air." By the time they get outside, he's got her. She's done for. I tell you, it's a crazy world, man.

According to Scott, GHB used to be sold in health food stores as a form of growth hormone stimulant or a sleep disorder medicine. It was taken off the shelves in 1991 when the Food and Drug Administration learned that GHB was being used by kids to get high. Scott says GHB is easy to produce; most GHB is produced in home labs or bathtubs, sometimes by kids ordering GHB kits off the Internet. They mix some nasty-sounding ingredients (engine degreaser, muratic acid, Drano, and some vinegar), and voila!—they produce a clear, odorless liquid that contains a salty taste.

GHB gives teens a stimulated-type high, but if they drink too much, they overdose. "GHB overdoses are the most incredible scenes you'll ever see in your life," said Scott. "Kids vomit, shake, then almost stop breathing. Their heart rates practically shut down. They look like they could die at any moment. They usually stay in this form of 'blackout' for three hours. When the drug starts to wear off, we call it the 'dawn syndrome,' the time they start coming out of it."

GHB is the drug to watch out for. Its initials stand for gamma hydroxybutyrate, but "grievous harm to the body" would be closer to the truth. The drug has been linked to at least sixty deaths since 1990 and more than 5,700 recorded overdoses, according to the Drug Enforcement Administration.

Sexual predators love GHB because it's the ultimate "date rape" drug. A discreet and undetected squeeze of the Visine bottle causes a girl to experience euphoria, hallucinations, followed by a deep sleep. She won't remember *anything*. That's when she can be taken advantage of—by several guys taking turns.

> I can't remember what happened that night. I woke up thirteen, fourteen hours later at a friend's house. Somebody told me I drank GHB and that what I did after that was consensual. Maybe it was; maybe it wasn't.
>
> —*Andrea*, age fifteen

"I've read hundreds of victim statements over the years," said Detective Scott. "The typical statement is a young woman or teen girl stating that she was hanging out at a rave or a nightclub, and then she met a guy with black hair named Johnny who asked her to dance. After the dance, he offered to buy her a drink, and the next thing she knew, she woke up under the fire escape with her clothes off and a pain in her thighs. I've also heard about instances in which a girl was at a non-alcohol establishment, drinking a Sprite, and then waking up under the same circumstances."

Sometimes young women never wake up. A fifteen-year-old girl in Detroit died after drinking a soda laced with GHB at a party. Four young men who caused her death were sentenced to prison terms ranging from five to fifteen years.

GHB has replaced rohypnol—or "roofies"—as the date-rape drug of choice. The laws against rohypnol are so severe that if you are arrested for having the drug in your possession, you're toast with the judicial system. Rohypnol and a date-rape

cousin called clonazepam cause amnesia, serious motor impair-
ment, and even respiratory failure. They're still prevalent
drugs because they're cheap—usually $1 each, which is why
they've earned the sobriquet "dollar date."

Looking for Teachable Moments

Chances are high, probably 80 percent or more, that your
teens use drugs regularly or experiment with them. Talking
with your children about drugs may not be as difficult as you
think. Children began learning about the dangers of drugs in
elementary schools through the DARE programs, and depic-
tions of drug use are pervasive throughout the entertainment
media. Your kids may think that their knowledge about drugs
is rather sophisticated.

Look for teachable moments to talk about drugs. A conversation could be jumpstarted by watching a *20/20* segment on
GHB, hearing drug-related lyrics on the car radio ("Lucy in the
sky with diamonds..."), or reading the sports page and learning
that yet another high-profile athlete was busted for drug use.

Let your teens hear where you stand. Talk about their
future, reminding them how drug use can ruin their chances
of being accepted into a good college or limit their career
choices. If they retort that taking drugs is a "victimless crime,"
remind them that there is a victim—the teen taking the drugs.

Ponder these questions as you consider whether your own
teens might be among those who use or experiment with drugs:

- On Friday and Saturday evenings, are your teens out with
  friends past 10 P.M. or a reasonable curfew?
- Do you go to sleep on weekend nights without witnessing
  their arrival home?
- Are you unfamiliar with their friends?

- Do they constantly ask you for more "allowance"?
- Have you noticed money missing from your purse or bill-fold?
- Do your teens sleep half the day away on Saturdays and Sundays?
- Have your teens' grades taken a nosedive in the last semester?
- Have they become more uncommunicative recently?
- Have your teens started dressing "differently"?

If you answered affirmatively to two or more questions, I suggest that you take your teens out for a restaurant meal and go through the Discussion Starter questions at the end of this chapter. I would not delay such a conversation. Helping your child as soon as you can may save you from some agonizing times down the road—and from an expensive "rehab" program, many of which are not covered by regular medical insurance.

What I am attempting to do in this chapter is show you that there are many more tempting drugs out there today than ever before. If you find pacifiers in your teen's room, she isn't practicing for motherhood or going through a second infancy. Often teens decide to send clear signals that they *want* you to know they are taking drugs. Listen in on this conversation I had with Kevin:

Sara: How did you start getting into trouble and doing drugs?

Kevin: I started getting into trouble when I was eleven years old. I became rebellious, stopped doing what my parents told me to do, and began smoking pot with my friends at Munn Park. My parents didn't really know what was going on for a long time.

Sara: But couldn't they tell you were on drugs?

Kevin: I'm really surprised that they didn't. I guess they didn't want to know. I basically told them; I told them without saying words. I showed them through my actions. Anybody who knew about drugs knew I was taking them.

Sara: So that was a mistake they made by not being educated on what kids are like when they're high on drugs?

Kevin: Yeah. They should have been educated.

Strategies to Get Them Off Drugs

I showed them through my actions. A very telling admission for both generations. If anything, you should be keeping a closer eye on children when they reach adolescence. Just because their voices change or they begin filling out a bikini doesn't mean that your parental role is over. It means it just got tougher!

If you suspect your children may be taking drugs, look for the root reasons. Why are your teens experimenting with drugs? What's the attraction? Why do they want to escape reality? Who are their friends? Remember peer pressure from your teenage days? Human nature hasn't changed in one generation.

Teach your kids that their bodies are temples that God created and that you don't harm the temple God has given you. What we've found at the House of Hope is that the root problem of drug use is spiritual. If teens have a reason larger than themselves not to take drugs and have hope in the future, they can get off the drugs.

Kids Still Smoke Up a Storm

I would be remiss if I didn't say anything about smoking. Most teens at the House of Hope arrive as smokers. Cigarettes were their companions to help pass the time. Dragging on a Marlboro is how they learned to relax or unwind, and it's not because they had a tough day learning long division.

There are deeper issues at work here. Maybe their parents weren't available for them when they needed a mother or father to talk to. This sounds silly, but cigarettes become a parent or friend. Kids light up when they're sad and need someone to talk to; they light up when they're happy and want to share their good fortune. Cigarettes become the friends they can hang out with any time they want. Smokes are always there for them, and after a few drags and inhalations of nicotine, smokers always feel better.

There are reasons why we have the vices that we have. We all use things to cope with life, whether it's eating food, watching TV, going to the mall to shop, or hanging out on the street corner and watching life pass by. Smoking is a coping mechanism for insecurity, which can mean that teens feel insecure when they are not spending enough time with their parents.

But let's say that you are spending time with your teens or that you have made the commitment to do so after reading this book. Your teen still smokes, and you would like him to quit this vile habit. I would start a conversation with him in this way: "Josh, we're going to start a new rule here. I know you're smoking. You know I don't want you to smoke, so I'm going to make it a little more difficult for you. You're not allowed to smoke in the house. I don't know what you're going to do down the street, but I don't want you to do it in the house or when we are doing things together as a family because I'm concerned about your health."

Here's something you can do to encourage your teen to quit, and it's something we've done with our House of Hope kids. Take a yellow Post-It note and write on it, "I love you and want the best for you." Stick or tape this note on his bathroom mirror so he can see it every morning when he washes up. He will feel your love, and his attitude will soften (at least, we hope it will). Continue to encourage your teenager with each small step he takes in kicking the habit.

We have great success in helping our teens quit smoking. I attribute that to positive peer pressure. When a smoking teen is around a couple of dozen teens who don't smoke, he finds that he doesn't need that cigarette as much as he thought he did. Your teen will listen with big ears when a peer tells him that he quit two months ago and his lungs are totally clear now.

As for your teens, who are they hanging out with? Do their buddies smoke? If they do, it's going to be very difficult not to puff with their friends. They may need a change of scenery!

Raised on Ritalin

AS HORRIBLE AS RECREATIONAL DRUGS ARE, there's another concern I must raise, and that's kids on prescription drugs. There is an explosion of young boys and girls, many who are still under the age of ten, who have been diagnosed with Attention Deficit Hyperactivity Disorder (ADHD) and depression. ADHD is defined broadly as inattention, impulsiveness, or hyperactivity that causes disruptions at home and in the classroom.

The solution? Medicate them. Give them Ritalin or Prozac. Drug them out.

Adolescents on antidepressant drugs are so commonplace that I would estimate that 80 percent of the teens arrive at the House of Hope on Ritalin or some other type of prescription drugs. But I often wonder if their parents rushed their out-of-control child to a doctor's office because they were unwilling or unable to discipline at home or because they wanted a quick fix for grade school rambunctiousness. Many suspect that we are simply drugging healthy children into submission.

> I started getting medicated when I was about six years old. I was always hyper in kindergarten—running out the door when the teacher told me not to, standing on my chair, talking when the teacher told me to be quiet. I even talked back to my mom when she told me to be quiet. A psychiatrist said I had Attention Deficit Hyperactivity Disorder, so he put me on Ritalin, twenty milligrams, three times a day. I've been on drugs like Ritalin for eight years—more than half of my life. Right now at the House of Hope, I'm on Depachode, Seroquel, and a bunch of different medications. Most of them are antidepressants.
>
> —*Ryan*, age fourteen

I mean no offense to the millions of parents raising children with legitimate hyperactivity issues, but I cannot but notice that the race to Ritalinize our kids is a disturbing national trend. The *Journal of the American Medical Association* reported in 2000 that the use of certain psychotropic drugs, antidepressants, and stimulants doubled or even tripled for preschoolers between the ages of two and four during the 1990s.

Why? Are we seeing more restlessness and inattentiveness in preschoolers because they are parked in day-care centers all day long and not at home with their mothers? Could be.

When these children reach elementary school, they continue to act out and disrupt classrooms, prompting school authorities to call a teacher-parent conference to discuss what to do about Johnny's "behavior issue." That's when you see parents and

Johnny beating a path to the door of least resistance—the doctor's office. They often leave with a drug prescription in hand.

I had to take a test to get on Ritalin. The doctor asked me questions like: "Do you hear voices in your head?" "When you move, does your head twitch?" My mom kept saying, "Yes, yes, and yes." So I was put on Ritalin, and it didn't do anything for me. In fact, it just made things worse. Ritalin made me sad, but I had to act happy. I had huge mood swings.

—*Katrina*, age sixteen

My father always said that children should be seen and not heard. When he left Mom and my life, I felt like his actions gave me free rein to do whatever I wanted to do. I became really loud and obnoxious, which adults saw as "attention problems." They thought my problems could be solved by a little magic pill. "Here, take this Ritalin, it'll be all right." I was told that I was a bipolar manic depressant, just like my father. My life became one nonstop roller coaster. When my doctor told me that I would be taking medication all my life, the news made me even more depressed. I asked myself, "What's wrong with me?"

—*Jamie*, age fourteen

When teens arrive at the House of Hope heavily medicated by prescription drugs (mainly Ritalin), we recognize that many *do* need these antidepressant drugs, at least at the outset. Most school-age children with ADHD—it's been estimated as high as 90 percent—respond well to treatment with these drugs. But some children clearly do not, and that's what we saw in

Wesley when he arrived at the House of Hope at age fourteen. Like Ryan earlier in this chapter, Wesley was always misbehaving in kindergarten. Wesley couldn't stay focused on one task for very long. School officials ran a battery of tests, then passed him on to a doctor who diagnosed Wesley with ADHD. The young child was put on Ritalin.

The antidepressant calmed down Wesley to some extent, but the prescription drug also zapped his appetite. When he reached third grade, Wesley weighed sixty pounds—twenty or thirty pounds underweight. When his mother expressed concern, they switched the child to Dexedrine. He continued to shed precious pounds.

They tried doubling the dosage, switching between the two drugs, and taking Ritalin and Dexedrine simultaneously. Nothing worked. Wesley continued to be very underweight for his age, even as he went through growth spurts. When Wesley's parents divorced when he was twelve years old, doctors added Adderall and Flexor to the mix. At age thirteen, Wesley weighed eighty-five sickly pounds. The poor lad was ingesting four different drugs each day.

Wesley began smoking pot when he became a teenager. The combination of cannabis and powerful antidepressants caused him to become violently ill one time. Once he passed out for three hours, which prompted a call to 911.

Wesley began selling some of his pills to school friends. They liked the buzz. One night he gulped down three "sheets" of Flexor—thirty pills in all—to see what it would be like. He threw up every day for two weeks and began shedding even more weight off his skinny frame. When Wesley arrived in our care, he was five feet, two inches tall and weighed ninety pounds.

He turned the corner at a summer camp for the House of Hope teens. "The counselors prayed that God would take away the reasons for me to take all my medicines," Wesley explained. "Within weeks, I was doing so well that my psychiatrist said I could stop taking my medicines. I started gaining weight and growing. Now I'm exactly what I'm supposed to be at five feet, seven inches and 145 pounds. I'm eating a lot these days. It was really cool that God could intervene like that."

God's ability to heal His children, along with loving discipline and counseling, has helped us see tremendous changes in youngsters like Wesley. In the House of Hope's history, I know of only two or three children from whom we could not totally remove the medication.

I'm a teacher for the girls' program at the House of Hope. When Colleen came to us, she couldn't sit for long periods of time or focus on her schoolwork. Though she was fourteen years old, she read at a third-grade level. We had to help her learn her phonics and syllables all over again.

As her emotional healing process began, we started to wean Colleen from Ritalin. We saw a tremendous improvement in her ability to concentrate on her schoolwork and in her reading and writing abilities. When children get diagnosed with ADHD these days, they get labeled. I think it's their emotional issues that keep them from being able to focus. I'm very sensitive to labeling youngsters. It's like giving them an excuse. Sure, there are learning challenges out there, and we all learn differently. But most of these labels do not prove to be true, at least from what I've seen in years of teaching school. Once you get in there and start working with the teenagers and encourage them, they eventually come out from under the stigmatizing labels that affect them emotionally. I once saw a young boy on five different drugs progress to the point where we could take him off his medication.

Each teen at the House of Hope works at his own pace on a curriculum popular with homeschoolers. Since adolescents come into the House of Hope and leave at different times, it would be very difficult to teach them in a single class setting. So we tutor them as they work through their workbooks. We always see an ability in them to focus.

—*Liz Clark*, a House of Hope teacher

We have kids arrive at the House of Hope carrying labels the size of anvils on their shoulders. The labels are: "You'll never amount to anything," or "You're nothing but a whore," or "Nobody wants you," or "You'll never do well in school."

Guess what? Kids have a way of fulfilling expectations. If they are tagged as "problem kids," they live up to those low expectations. They quit trying in the classroom and at home. When they quit trying, they begin acting out because they are seeking attention. They are saying, *Look at me! I can be somebody!* If they can't get positive reinforcement, they'll find a way to get it negatively.

All too often, school authorities and parents take the path of least resistance: an ADHD diagnosis and subsequent Ritalin prescription. Yes, this approach is merited sometimes, but in so many of our kids? Our policy at the House of Hope is "Time and hugs—not drugs." It works.

If you think one of your children may have an attention deficit problem, ask yourself: Does my son (or daughter) have an attention deficit from me? This is a tough, thought-provoking question, but if you answer it honestly, you'll know what you ought to do.

Discussion Starters

If your child is on Ritalin or some other therapeutic drug:

Do you know any other kids on Ritalin?

What do they say about taking that drug? Does it help them?

What do you think about Ritalin? Do you think Ritalin helps you?

What do you think we could do to get you off Ritalin?

Is that something you'd like to work toward?

If your child is not on Ritalin or some other therapeutic drug:

Do you have any friends on Ritalin?

How many kids in your class are on drugs like Ritalin?

What happens to them when they stop taking the drug?

How does the drug affect them? Did you notice any differences in them?

Watch Out for Those Daisy Dukes!

JEANS WITH BELL-BOTTOMS the size of manhole covers. Flaming red tube tops that announce she's bustin' out all over. Guys wearing pants that sag so much you can see the "plumber's crack." Bare midriffs and daisy dukes.

The way teens dress can frustrate parents no end, not to mention the libido of teen guys, who aren't known for turning a blind eye to the female form or bare skin. As for parental frustration, let's listen in on a conversation between Jerry, a parent of two teenagers, and Jessica, one of our able counselors here at the House of Hope:

Jerry: Thank you, Jessica, for meeting with me because I need some explanation of the way teen girls dress today. When I drop my son and daughter off at a dance, I can't help but notice a swoop of giggly girls wearing skin-tight spandex and spaghetti strap tops with their bra straps showing. I think the way they dress is ridiculous. Can I tell my kids what to wear?

Jessica: In principle, you can tell them what to wear, but whether they listen to you is another matter.

Jerry: But my daughter says she wants to wear those bare midriff things.

Jessica: My question to you would be: Where did she get them? Who purchased them for her?

Jerry: I guess my wife.

Jessica: If so, you have a parenting issue. You and your wife need to be on the same catalog page. You need to come to an understanding of what that type of dressing does to guys. You, as a man, could speak to your wife and explain what skimpy outfits do to rev up a man's motor. A revealing dress doesn't affect women the same way it affects men because men are visually stimulated. Maybe you could help your wife to understand that those revealing clothes *are* a big deal. Those clothes could get your daughter into a bad situation sooner or later.

Jerry: My wife thinks Michelle looks cute in halter-tops that could have been handed out at Hooters. Believe me, I haven't forgotten what *I* was thinking about when I saw that type of clothing in my teen years!

Jessica: Right. This is something that you have to be careful with. Some girls know what they're doing, and they dress that way to get the looks from the boys. Others dress that way because their peers do. Either way, this leads me to ask you this question: Why does she need to get the looks? I think Michelle understands what she's doing. So why does she need somebody to look at her?

Jerry: You mean she may be craving attention?

Jessica: I think she's craving male attention. A father can satisfy that need for male attention.

Jerry: So you're saying it's a father issue.

Jessica: Right again. Which would lead me to ask you this: What role are you playing in her life?

Jerry: Are you saying that girls who dress that way want attention or love from their fathers?

Jessica: Nine times out of ten. I've counseled too many girls over the years who've told me that their fathers come home from work, grab the TV zapper, and never become interested in them or their lives. Then you have situations in which the father is an absentee parent or a removed father. Kids tell me, "My dad left us," "He's an alcoholic," or "He wasn't around. We got by without him." Another one I hear a lot is, "Yeah, my dad was around, but he just worked a lot. He was a good dad. He provided for the family and never hit me. But I wouldn't say that he was involved in my life."

Jerry: It can't be all my fault. I'm trying to do something about this, but my wife says Michelle looks cute that way. You said I should talk to my wife first.

Jessica: Realistically, your wife should be in here for counseling. Then I would turn to her and say, "Do you understand what this is doing?" I would also regard what she is wearing. I have met many moms who wear tight, short outfits, but that's not good since it's a seductive thing. If Michelle comes out of her room in a little tube top and skin-tight pants, she is basically bait for some older guy.

Jerry: Bait? How do I handle this?

Jessica: By talking to her. Let her know how you feel, but not in a one-sided manner. I would just say something like this, "Michelle, when you leave the house dressed like that, what you're really doing is putting yourself out there like bait. I don't want to see you get hurt. I care for you. I want the best for you. I'm expressing my concern because there are consequences in the real world for dressing so sexy. Revealing clothes 'communicate' in ways that you never thought possible. Guys will think you are available to have sex with them."

Remember, however, that your daughter is becoming her own person. If she *really* wants to, she can disregard your advice. But your voice should ring inside her mind as she runs into guys who try to hit on her.

Jerry: What do you think is appropriate dress for teen girls?

Jessica: What I'm about to say comes from my personal beliefs and the morals that I hold. First of all, I think you can go to an extreme on this clothes issue. I'm not really for either extreme, but I do think that if something that a girl is wearing is causing a boy to look at her in a, well, lustful way, then it's probably too tight or too short. Take the halters and the tube tops. I'm not a man, but I've worked with enough men and boys to know that those kinds of tops can immediately take things to a sexual level. The moral issue is that dressing that way is causing others to go to places they don't need to go. There's always going to be one in the bunch that takes it to that extent every single time, no matter what you're wearing. A girl could wear a turtleneck and some kid would get turned on. I'm talking about just your normal, run-of-the-mill, average guys.

I think the short skirts and the daisy duke shorts—Raggedy Ann type cutoffs—are too much for most guys, however. The daisy dukes literally just cover right up to the top of the leg, and most of the time you've got butt cheeks hanging outside. Daisy dukes are frequently worn with a little spaghetti strap top or cropped top that's see-through. Those tops, made of meshy material, are usually worn without a bra.

Jerry: Is the no-bra look coming back?

Jessica: I don't know what planet you've been on, but the no-bra look *is* back. The daisy dukes don't cover enough. I don't know whether people up north wear them because it's too cold much of the year. It just goes to show that we see the craziest things in warm-weather Orlando. I'm sure they do in California as well. Daisy dukes cover just enough so that you can't get into trouble for being exposed.

Jerry: Let's talk about how the guys dress. What kind of standards do you have here at the House of Hope for the boys? Can their pants sag?

Jessica: We have the two-inch rule here, which means the pants cannot be any more than two inches larger than the boy's waist size. In other words, if he has a 29 waist, the pants can't be any larger than size 31. The boys also have to wear belts, and the pants can't sag down to the point where their boxers or briefs show. Our boys complain that this look makes them look like "preps."

Jerry: Preps?

Jessica: Yes, preps as in preppies. Preps wear khaki pants, usually Dockers with white button-up shirts or plaid button-ups. They wear an oxford blue or brown buck kind of shoes. Kids call this the "Gap" look or the "Abercrombie & Fitch" look. They top things off with a baseball cap, especially if they are jocks.

Then you have the 'hood look in which kids wear these big sweatshirts and pullovers with hoods on them. They have huge pants, usually the Jinco brand, that sag like no tomorrow. I think the deal is to wear the pants low enough so that they come right below the bottom of their butts so all their boxers show. I've seen kids belt their pants below the middle of their thighs to hold them up. The pants usually bunch at the bottom. They wear combat boots or Doc Marten-type boots. Some of the fitted pants have bell-bottoms that are just huge! We had a girl here at the House of Hope whose cuffs were 33 inches around!

Not all girls wear the baggy jeans. We've had girls wear jeans that were so skin tight that they had to lie down on the bed to zip them up or button them. They certainly showed every single curve, which makes them just as bad as the daisy dukes. When I point that out to them, they say, "But they're long enough!" They just miss the point.

Jerry: So as a parent, is there a middle ground here, or do I just refuse to buy?

Jessica: You can refuse to buy, yes, by all means. But you'll get into a problem when she turns sixteen or seventeen and goes to Publix and gets a job sacking groceries. Then she can buy clothes on her own. What you want to do is show leadership in these clothes issues. Good parental leaders have good relationships with their teens. In building your relationship you can say, "Hey, listen, this is what happens to boys when you wear those clothes."

If this "hey, listen" comes from the dad, that's a good thing because you're a man. You should know what you're talking about when it comes to what gets a guy's motor out of neutral. The problem with saying, "You cannot wear this" is that teens sneak out the clothes they want to wear in a plastic bag and then change into them after they've gone to their friends' houses. Or they put whatever they want to wear underneath a big sweatshirt, which they take off when they arrive where they are going.

Jerry: Are you saying that I can't ban my daughter from wearing certain types of clothes?

Jessica: Not at all. If "talking" about it doesn't work and you feel that your father-daughter relationship is on a good foundation, then you should confront your daughter, but not in an angry way. "Michelle, I have to tell you that I really don't want you wearing that revealing tube top. I'm saying this for your own protection. There are too many guys waiting to take advantage of you because that tube top sends the wrong message."

Maybe this is just a side note, but I think there's an underlying issue that goes back to love without discipline. You discipline your daughter out of love—because you care for her. She can't see the whole picture yet. Besides, if you don't say something, who will? Your daughter is depending on you, although it may be years before she understands why and how you had her best interests at heart.

A Fair Compromise

At the House of Hope, we have standards for the teens while giving them some freedom of expression. Jessica mentioned our "two inch rule," in which the boys (and girls, actually) cannot wear pants more than two inches larger than their normal waist size. We think that is a fair compromise, especially for the boys who complain that regular-fitting pants "cut" into them.

I expressed who I was by the clothes I wore. I fit into a clique by the way I dressed. I hung out with the "arts" crowd—we liked to dress in bright colors because we wanted to be loud and look stupid. We all wore Chuck Taylor Converse sneakers in different colors: black, red,

and white. Then there were the jocks. They wore their
football uniforms five days a week. The preppies—they
wore pleated Dockers, button-up shirts from A & F or
collared shirts from Tommy Hilfiger, with a Nike cap
and $180 Nikes that their parents bought for them. The
girls wore American Eagle and Lerners, stuff from Anne
Taylor, like beige cardigans and brown sandals. They
looked so shallow to me. Then there was the drugged-
out clique, who wore whatever clothes were closest to
the bed. Punks wore whatever they wanted, like 7-11
shirts and McDonald's hats.

—Jay, age seventeen

We try to teach our girls modesty, and generally speaking,
the girls work with us. I think that girls who expose a lot of
their bodies do so because they have such a poor self-concept.
They think this is the only way to get attention. It can work
the other way as well: girls will sometimes dress like guys in an
attempt to hide who they are. I remember a girl who
came into the program wearing guy clothes all the time—
baggy pants, huge shirts. As Stephanie received healing in her
life, we saw her change and begin wearing more feminine
things. Her graduation from the House of Hope prompted her
to put on an evening gown. Stephanie was absolutely gorgeous.

What does this mean for parents? It means you will have to
be involved with the clothes your teens choose or buy. I would
even suggest that you offer to take your teen shopping for
clothes, adopting a cheerful attitude of "let's find something
cute" and not "don't even try one of the low-cut tops."

There's a line between accentuating the positive and being
brazen about your sexuality. Far be it from me to describe

where that line is, but almost everyone knows when that line is crossed. Dresses, tops, and shirts *can* show a girl's figure in a way that doesn't look like a sexual come-on.

I understand how some boys don't identify with the preppie look, which is fine. At the House of Hope, we promote modest and appropriate dress for our teens. The following rules can be adjusted by staff, but we think they are inherently reasonable. How do they match up with your family standards? Could you adopt these guidelines in your family?

- Clothes must be neat and modest.
- Underwear must be worn always. Girls must wear bras and underwear.
- No sexy underwear or thongs are permitted.
- Girls may not wear boy's clothing or underwear. Boys may not wear girl's clothing or underwear.
- Make-up, perfume, cologne, and nail polish must be used sparingly and with good judgment.
- Bathing suits must be modest. At the House of Hope, no bikinis may be worn. One-piece suits for the girls cannot be of the "dental floss" variety. Boys must wear loose-fitting suits.
- Boys must wear shirts always, except when they are swimming.
- Shorts must be of modest length. Girls may not wear short shorts ("daisy dukes").
- Skirts and dresses must be of modest length. When kneeling, a skirt must come within two inches of the ground.
- Bra straps must not show, and blouses must be loosely fitted.
- No cropped blouses are allowed. All blouses must be long enough to cover the stomach and must reach pants—with arms lifted up.

- Pants may not drag on the ground and must be of a reasonable length.

There's another thing you should know about teen dress: The statement "Clothes make the man (or the woman)" never rings truer than during the adolescent years. Their eyes are also judging, always taking measure. Teens are slaves to certain brands, and they all know what's cool and what isn't.

> Kids spent a lot of money on clothes. I know I did. I had huge pants with balloon vests with glitter everywhere. I used to spend an hour getting ready every night to go to the clubs. I painted my face with glow-in-the-dark paint because it was cool.
>
> What wasn't cool were the kids whose parents kept them in the eighties. They were the ones who wore screen-print T-shirts that had little bunnies on them. They were the ones who wore green shorts that go up to here with Jimmy Z shirts. Maybe their parents told them how to dress, or maybe they didn't have the money to buy the right clothes. What I do know is that they hung out together because no one wanted to be seen with them.
>
> —*Marissa*, age sixteen

Letting your teens purchase the "right clothes" isn't necessarily a bad thing (even we all had to have certain brands as we grew up), but you can still set standards here as well. In recent years, Abercrombie & Fitch and Calvin Klein have embarked on sexually charged advertising themes that have been more about child pornography than about selling clothes. Next time, show the offending magazine advertisement to your teens and ask what they think. What message is being sold? What's behind this ad?

The answers should be illuminating.

Discussion Starters

What are some of the new popular styles on campus these days?

What are your favorite clothes?

What are your favorite brands?

Do girls have to watch what they wear?

Do girls' clothes affect how guys think about them?

Tell me what someone looked like when they wore immodest clothes.

What do guys look like when they are dressed inappropriately?

5

The Goth Look

WHEN JASON CAME TO THE HOUSE OF HOPE, he didn't pack his black eyeliner with him. He also left behind white pancake makeup and his Doc Marten black boots—knee-high, front-lace leather boots that would have done a Nazi proud. The rest of his extensive all-in-black wardrobe stayed behind as well.

Jason was a goth, a term you may have heard since it was linked with the two boys who shot and killed their classmates at Columbine High School in Littleton, Colorado. Goths are all about attitude, style, and a way of thinking about life—and death. Many goths are consumed with apocalyptic fantasies, including Jason, who, at the age of thirteen, had adopted the "doomcookie" look of the gothic subculture: black shirt, black stovepipe pants, $150 Doc Marten black boots that nearly reached his kneecaps, black lipstick, and black eyeliner.

Sometimes he and his gothic friends, including guys, used white powder on their faces along with their black eyeliner and lipstick. Their ghastly look gave them the appearance of dead bodies, but that figures since goths worship death. Their obsession with darkness, depression, and death offers disaffected teens a sense of belonging.

That's why they slavishly follow the goth dress code right down to their name-brand boots and black fashion statements. You can also see their fixation on doom and gloom in their jewelry. Silver jewelry is popular with goths since it is a colder-looking precious metal than gold. Goths adorn themselves with silver bats, ankhs, coffins, pentagrams, and even crucifixes, the latter because they take a perverse joy in being sacrilegious. They paint cheap costume earrings black with silver accents. They love vampire trappings and the sense that they operate on society's fringes. Some goths are *really* out there: they participate in Satanism and vampirism, which could include ceremonial bloodletting. They will drink blood as a sort of spiritual communion.

Goths claim to appreciate the dichotomy of life, the contrast between light and dark, the difference between good and evil, and an awareness that the two can't exist without each other. Much of this thinking is superficial and pretentious, and even the goths know it. Those who consider themselves "true goths" look down upon those whom they consider to be *poseurs*. They steadfastly claim that their lifestyle is a harmless form of self-expression, but I see things differently: Goths seek the morbid underbelly of life and revel in darkness because they can't stand the light of truth.

Jason was caught up in this dark and perverse culture that loves shocking the adult population with its all-black dress and gloomy outlook on life. "Gothic was who I was," said Jason, who's now fifteen years old. "I was tired of being what everybody else wanted me to be. Gothic was dressing all in black and hanging out with friends who dressed in the same way."

Jason didn't have very many friends, but then again, the weirdness of the gothic culture doesn't engender many close relationships. Jason said he wore eyeliner to school but not black lipstick because he didn't want to draw *too* much attention to himself. Of course, a boy wearing eyeliner to school and not expecting anyone to notice is like a well-built girl wearing a plunging neckline and not expecting any boys to look at her.

Jason was noticed, all right, but it wasn't the kind of attention he was bargaining for. "Wearing black lipstick had a way of creating negative attention at school," Jason said. "People would say, 'Look at that freak,' or 'Oh, you must be gay.' Stuff like that. It didn't matter to me because I had been mocked all my life." But his hurting eyes told me he *did* mind being harassed and rejected.

Of the two thousand kids at Jason's school, perhaps a hundred dressed gothic. They didn't all hang out with each other because the gothic culture is full of petty jealousies and rivalries. Some were peaceful; others wanted to act out their pent-up frustrations against the world. When I asked Jason what he and his gothic buddies did for fun, he replied, "We hung out, did a lot of drugs, listened to music. My favorite band was Tool. Their music was mostly about death and hating people—especially Christians. That was fine with me because I knew some very religious people who weren't really Christians but said they were. They pointed their fingers and made fun of me."

If this is sounding a bit familiar, this is supposedly what the ostracized teens, Eric Harris and Dylan Klebold, felt at Columbine High School in the Denver suburb of Littleton. The two teenagers, who shot and killed thirteen students and one teacher and seriously injured a dozen more, belonged to a clique of brooding students called the Trench Coat Mafia. These troubled teens were fascinated with the occult, the nihilist shock rocker Marilyn Manson, and even Adolf Hitler (Harris and Klebold timed their deadly attack for April 19, 1999, the 110th anniversary of Hitler's birthday).

Harris and Klebold felt like outcasts among their peers, just like goths. John, one of our teenagers at the House of Hope, told me goths really bugged him. "There was this park where the goths hung out, maybe ten or fifteen of them," said John. "They would be down there doing their thing. You'd see all these people with their high boots and painted fingernails, guys who wore lipstick on their faces. I used to walk by them and think they were dogs."

When They Dress in Black

Kids caught up in the gothic culture are not dogs, but they are teens with emotions running high. Also running high is the blood pressure of parents who are shocked the first time their son or daughter dresses in black from head to toe and empties a bottle of black nail polish on their fingers and toes.

When I asked Josh, one of our seventeen-year-olds, what parents should do if their son buys an all-black wardrobe and a pair of Doc Martens, he replied, "There's nothing you can really tell a parent because if kids want to do that, they will do it. My parents tried to stop me, but they couldn't."

"What did they do to try to stop you?" I asked.

"They took away my clothes and threw them away. But I'd steal new ones from different people."

The first thing you—the parent—need to do is take a deep breath and think through a few questions. Why is your son or daughter dressing that way? Why is he feeling "dark" about himself? Are you spending enough time with your child? Are you fighting every day? Are you telling your child she is stupid?

Goth teens may appear happy on the outside, but the fact that they've chosen to step out of the mainstream is a signal that they feel lonely, unappreciated, and unloved. Many carry suicidal thoughts, if for no reason other than because they listen to songs that glorify the "final solution" to their problems.

When teens arrive at the House of Hope, they understand that the gothic clothes don't come with them. "The kids that I've seen involved in goth seem to have a darkness about them," said Randy, a House of Hope counselor. "Initially, we just develop a relationship with them by loving them and caring for them. I said to one teen guy, 'Look, man, I don't know what's going on with you, but you seem "dark." There's stuff going on here that seems very scary and out of character for you. I just want you to know that we're going to work with you and love you.'"

Another thing you should know is that the gothic subculture is linked with many occult activities. I mentioned the ceremonial bloodletting and other occult behavior earlier, but let me give you a graphic example of what falling into the occult can do to someone. If you grew up in the Northeast in the mid-1970s, there's a good chance you remember the Son of Sam, a.k.a. David Berkowitz, who terrorized New York City for eighteen panic-filled months in 1976 and 1977. His string of shootings killed six people and seriously injured seven. Life became so scary that some women changed hair color or cut their hair because they thought the killer preferred a certain hairstyle or color of hair.

What was so frightening about the Son of Sam was the way he randomly approached male and female victims as they sat on their brownstone stoops or in their parked cars, pointed a .44 caliber pistol, and fired at point-blank range. The New York tabloids had a heyday with this gripping story until Berkowitz's dramatic arrest.

The Son of Sam was eventually convicted and sentenced to life in prison. What made him kill all those people?

We will never know for sure. But Berkowitz told Mike Yorkey, who's assisting me with this book, that he was always in trouble growing up. He fought in the schoolyard or stood up in the middle of class and started screaming at the teacher. A school counselor recommended to his parents that he see a child psychologist in Manhattan every week.

Despite his horrible behavior, his parents—especially his mother—showed David love. But when his mother died of lung cancer the fourteen-year-old teen became angry and self-destructive. He started vandalizing buildings. He felt a powerful urge to damage and destroy things. He experimented with alcohol and drugs, especially the psychedelic LSD. He was intensely drawn to all occult-related, satanic, and horror movies. Somehow he managed to graduate from high school, followed by an enlistment in the U.S. army for a three-year stint. When he was discharged in 1974, he came back to the Bronx and discovered that his friends had moved away from the neighborhood. David was lonely. Then one day he was invited to a party.

They were standing around this guy's apartment not doing much, when one of them said, "Hey, we got some friends who meet in a park nearby. Whaddya say we go check it out?"

Everyone went over to Pelham Bay Park in the Bronx and walked deep into the woods, where they found a couple dozen people drinking around a small fire.

Some were singing, and then they started chanting.

"What's this all about?" David asked someone dressed in black.

"Didn't anyone tell you we're pagans and witches?"

"No, they didn't," he replied.

They began asking him questions, checking him out, and then they invited David to return. They introduced him to satanism and their rituals. They drew pentagrams in the dirt and called upon the demonic powers. David said he felt this surge of energy come upon him, and he liked that feeling.

He purchased a satanic bible, and just holding that black book gave him paranormal powers. He developed psychic abilities, which freaked out his friends. "I remember walking up to a busy intersection, and I just knew there was going to be a car accident at the corner," he said. "So I waited, and sure enough, a minute or two later two cars piled into each other. It was so uncanny, and I visualized the whole incident in advance."

He dabbled more and more into satanism until the day he was asked to join the group. Just one hitch: a satanic priest took him aside and said he needed a family photo.

"Why's that?"

"Listen, we want you to join, but we have a policy," said the priest. "You must provide a photo of some of your family members. We do this to protect ourselves because if you ever leave and go tell anybody about us, we will know who your family is, and we will hurt them. Everything has its price."

David believed the priest's words. For months, he had witnessed animal sacrifices to appease the powers of darkness, but now they were being told that they had to be ready to make the quantum leap: human sacrifices. At least that's what Samhain—one of the highest-ranking demons—told them. They were soldiers of Samhain, which was abbreviated to Sam. That's really how David became known as the "Son of Sam," and he made a complete surrender to these powers of darkness.

Some type of demonic entity entered his body. He believed he was a soldier in Satan's army, and he and his cohorts were determined to bring New York City to its knees through a reign of terror. They began with vandalism and arson. Their group deliberately set around two thousand fires. David quickly passed the threshold from casual participant to actual devil worshipper. Once he willingly gave the devil his body and his mind, the next step seemed logical: he would become a killing machine and shed innocent blood. "I can't explain why I did what I did, but I now know that those actions caused much grief in many families," said David.

What a sad, sad story for the victims and their families. That's why I implore you not to discount the power of the occult or satanism. If you find trappings of satanic worship in your teen's bedroom (for instance, a satanic bible), you have every right to be alarmed! This will require the involvement of a local church pastor or therapist. I beg you not to let a day go by because occult ritual demands bloodshed.

Not a Passing Fad

Let's return to the gothic scene, since that is more common than occult behavior these days. Much of the goth scene is about a sense of belonging, so if your teen is already hanging out with gothic friends, it will be difficult for him to abandon them. You may hope that their penchant for dressing up in goth is a passing fad, but I would be wary of holding on tightly to that point of view. Gothic kids are a cause for alarm because their dress and their mannerisms are a symptom of a more serious, underlying problem. Goths are looking for experiences in other places because they are spending very little time with you—their parents. The relationship is not there.

Look beneath her appearance and ask yourself if you are spending enough time with her. What changed in her life? When did she start dressing as a goth? How did these changes become apparent?

The answer is not banning those clothes. You have to get to the root of the problem, which could be feeling rejection from you, not spending enough time with you, dealing with hurts in her life, or trying to find an alternative way to get attention. It's really about seeking acceptance even if her dress shocks you, your friends, and the people she comes into contact with.

Turning her around depends on how quickly you get to the root of the problem. Once kids feel love and acceptance here at the House of Hope, and feel the security that comes with regular meals, unconditional love, normal school hours, and healthy family interaction, their desire to dress goth evaporates almost overnight.

Discussion Starters

Are there any goth kids at school?

Are they accepted, or are they outcasts?

Are goths into dark things and the occult?

Do you think the kids who did the Columbine shooting were goths?

What do you think of the goth look? Is it cool to you?

If you dressed like a goth, what should I do as a parent?

6

Music to Their Ears

WE THOUGHT WE'D BE DIFFERENT, didn't we?

Twenty, thirty years ago, when our parents let us listen to the car radio blaring "Jumping Jack Flash" by the Rolling Stones or "Do You Think I'm Sexy?" by Rod Stewart, we invariably heard them mutter, "That music is awful! You can't even understand the words!"

We vowed that when *we* had kids, we would be more libertarian regarding music. We couldn't imagine not liking the music our children would like. Then rap was invented (just a joke). Seriously, we were weaned on rock 'n' roll, rhythm and blues, disco, country, metal, and other kinds of music, and our brain cells remained *intact*. That's why we decided we would allow our kids to listen to popular music because we *understood* their desire to follow their musical heroes, who assume larger-than-life personas.

But something changed over the years. Popular music didn't die, as Don McLean sang in "American Pie," but it sure drove the Chevy to the levee and proceeded to sink underneath its own weight. Music morphed into a frenetic, bass-driven sound accented by raunchy lyrics that are played so loudly and so often that no one blushes anymore.

Rap music is one of the worst offenders. Rappers, in their stylized monotone, jive-talk about "bustin' bitches" and "hos," and employ street terms to describe oral sex, anal sex, and rape. They put down anything that's good, and they glorify cop killing and drug dealing. Kids lap it up because it's antiauthority.

> There's no question that music is the number-one influencer of teens. Just looking at a musical artist and his video tells you so much about the culture. There's a lot of sex, megasex. There's a lot of anger. There's a lot of four-letter words. I guess you could say that music's gotten uglier in the last twenty years.
>
> —*Frank*, a House of Hope counselor

Music is a powerful medium, ranking right up there with cinema. You don't think so? The next time you're alone in the car, turn on an "oldies" station and sing along to an old favorite. Although you haven't heard the song in decades, you'll remember the words like it was yesterday!

As with most art forms, music is extremely powerful with teenagers because it moves them to do something. Dr. Richard Pellegrino, a brain specialist who serves as a consultant to the entertainment industry, wrote in *Billboard* magazine that music interacts powerfully, often subconsciously, with receptors in the brain to produce "endorphin highs." He added that music triggers a flood of emotions and images that "have the ability to instantaneously produce very powerful changes in emotional states."

Concluded Dr. Pellegrino: "Take it from a brain guy: In twenty-five years of medicine, I still cannot affect a person's state of mind the way that one simple song can." Music shapes attitudes, points teens toward certain behaviors, and molds their worldviews at a time when they lack experience and maturity.

As is typical for teens, their inexperience is compensated for by their emotions and energy. Music artists have learned to feed on that energy by producing faster and faster music: the guiding principle is the quicker, the better. Bands such as Limp Bizkit, Korn, Marilyn Manson, Silverchair, Alice in Chains, KISS, and Godsmack know how to push the right buttons.

Today's music reflects this gotta-have-it-now mentality prevalent in our culture. Everything has to be instant these days—instant food, instant drinks, and instant access to the Internet. Have you noticed the foot race to increase bandwidth and download speeds off the Net? Web surfing is too slow for today's teens. When a faster computer hits the streets, teens want to purchase a new one because faster is better.

They want a faster processor because songs can be downloaded from the Internet and passed from friend to friend. Your teens may be downloading music from MP3 or Napster and "burning" a CD without your ever knowing it. Anyone with a computer connected to the Internet can download any kind of music he wants, usually free of charge.

Some Perspective, Please

Before I go much further, some perspective is called for. Your
generation had a style of music. The generation before you had
a style. Today's generation has a style—a style that may cause
you to switch the station on your car radio—but a style nonetheless. Tomorrow's generation will have a music style all its own.
Think of style as the way you like to have your eggs. Maybe you
grew up with Denver omelets and can't eat eggs any other way.
Maybe your kids prefer guacamole and salsa on scrambled eggs.
Is either taste wrong? Of course not. We're talking about personal preferences, which are usually formed in our youth.

Sometimes your personal music style is determined by
where you grow up. If you were raised in Texas twenty years
ago, your radio was probably tuned to Merle Haggard and
Dolly Parton. That's all changed now. Texas kids, for instance,
have a broader spectrum to choose from today thanks to
MTV, Web access, and increased marketing from record companies. Country music is now popular north of the Mason-
Dixon line, not just in the South.

"I know there will be certain styles that parents don't like,"
said Randy, a House of Hope counselor. "There's certain
music I don't like. The key is to find out what's happening
with your teens, who they're hanging out with, and where
they like to go. You've got to get a clearer picture and ask,
'Where is my child at regarding the pop scene? Where is my
child going in his likes and dislikes with music?'"

The key question for parents is *content*, not style. My issue
with popular music is not so much the beat but what the lyrics
say. If you're zapping through channels with your family and
stop on MTV long enough to say, "Look at those guys. They
look like girls!" or "I can't understand the words," all you've

done is reveal your prejudices or your age. What you're going to have to do is understand those words. And that's a very easy chore these days. Nearly all CDs come with lyrics printed on small booklets; no artists bother trying to hide their sexist, pro-anarchy, or profane language.

CDs also come with parental notification stickers, not that these do any good. I think a "PA" sticker actually *boosts* sales because kids gravitate to material that pokes a thumb into the eye of authority. Their thinking: *If it's bad, then it has to be good.*

Another thing that is a problem in many households is concerts. What should parents do when their son wants to attend a Marilyn Manson concert? Let's listen to this conversation between a father named Robert, and Randy, a House of Hope counselor:

Robert: My son wants to go to the Marilyn Manson concert next month. He told me that he purchased tickets with his own money. I don't know much about Marilyn Manson. What should I do?

Randy: You don't know much about Marilyn Manson? Then you need to take a cram course, and while you're at it, you need to bone up on other groups that your son is drawn to. Once you learn more about the groups and their music and lyrics, then you will understand what your child is being exposed to. Once you learn what Marilyn Manson is singing about—death, drugs, and sex—you won't be so inclined to allow him to attend the concert.

Robert: Does that mean I should tell him that he can't go?

Randy: You will have to make that determination since you are the parent. But I will say this: you are responsible for what you allow your child to do.

Ideally, the time to talk to your child about whether he can go to the Manson concert is *before* he purchases the ticket. But for sake of argument, let's say that you find out after learning that he spent $35 on a floor-level seat. If you feel strongly that he should not go (because of the violent and sacrilegious nature of his songs), then I would bite the bullet and offer to buy his ticket from him. (Of course, if he can sell it to a friend, fine.) Establishing a principle—"Next time, you will have to check with us before you buy a concert ticket"—is well worth the cost of a single ducat to a Marilyn Manson concert.

I recommend that you enact a similar policy when it comes to buying music. If your teen wants to purchase the new Manson CD or Madonna's latest offering, I would say something like this: "Patrick, let's go down to the Wherehouse together and listen to Marilyn Manson's new CD. We can check out the lyrics together. We can also discuss what his message is and decide if that's something you really need to be pumping into your brain."

You can expect a tussle. Your children will say, "But you don't trust me." Trust me, they'll say it. But stick to your guns and give every indication that you want to be open-minded and fair. If you discover that the music is violent, ugly, and drops F-words throughout its lyric booklet, calmly remind them that you are responsible to protect them from those influences. Say something like, "I'm sorry, Patrick, but the new Marilyn Manson CD doesn't meet the family standard. One day you'll be making your own choices about music, but that day hasn't arrived yet."

Colored by Drugs

There is one more thing you should know about today's music, which, I will admit, is not very "accessible" to the ears of anyone over forty years old. While today's teens prefer their own style of music, their preference is often colored by drugs. I'll let Serena explain what I mean:

When I hit the teen years, the music really got on my nerves at first. I didn't understand it, and I thought it was obnoxious. But when I got into drugs and drinking, music started sounding better to me. I found music is to be filtered around the drugs. It was like they made the music to enhance my high.

For instance, with acid they make the music to have little sounds in the background that aren't a steady beat but a chopped-up beat. When your mind is altering and wondering where the sound came from, that beat enhances the drug. Then they'll have the lights go with the music, which messes you up even more. With ecstasy and drinking, the beat that comes out of it enhances the roll of the drug and its longevity.

I'll never forget going into a club in Cocoa Beach for the first time. I was on ecstasy and acid when the laser light show came on. I saw this guy come out with lasers in his hands and a custom-made unit that made it look like lasers were coming out of his eyes. Two DJs were spinning behind him. The laser man moved his eyes and his hands to the beat of the music. In my drug-altered state, I thought he *was* the music. Techno music helped keep me steady.

I can tell you this. If I were listening to classic rock and on ecstasy at the same time, it would ruin my whole roll. Classic rock just doesn't have the beat for being on ecstasy.

The need to listen to music to enhance the drug experience is the reason why today's teens are attracted to rap, techno, and a type of music called "house," "jungle," or "ace." They have steady, monotonous beats that appeal to kids high on drugs and keep them in a good mood. They want to dance and move around the whole time. When they're not on drugs, the songs have a way of taking them back to their formerly altered states. Kids tell me that fast techno music makes cocaine and crack a better experience, but teens on heroin are too zonked out to really care what's coming over the speakers.

> When I was in Orlando at the Firestone Club, I had taken too many pills. I just lay down because I couldn't stand up anymore. There was a speaker next to the couch that I lay down on, so the boom-boom of the bass kept me awake. I thought I was going crazy while laying on that couch. I had these weird dreams about elephants floating through the sky. Deer talked to me. Some friends took me home, but during the drive, I kept telling my friends not to hit the deer in the middle of Interstate 4. "The deer says he loves you," I said. My friends kept asking me what I was talking about.
>
> —*Rachel*, age seventeen

Let me offer some alternatives. I don't think it does anyone any good to throw up their hands and ban music that kids like. There are alternatives—great gospel and CCM artists—that you can plug your kids into. CCM, which stands for Contemporary Christian Music, has tons of groups and singers in nearly every genre—rap, pop, rock, metal, ska, and techno. Some CCM artists are very "edgy," but you can count on positive lyrics that lift you up rather than bring you down.

Groups and artists that we can recommend are dc Talk, Steven Curtis Chapman, Bleach, Rebecca St. James, Jars of Clay, Switchfoot, Audio Adrenaline, Newsboys, Dogwood, and Geoff Moore and the Distance. You may not like the beat, but at least your kids won't be listening to "dark" music about rebellion, suicide, and no hope for the future.

So have your teens listen to some positive alternatives at your local music store. Who knows? They may come back humming a new tune.

Discussion Starters

Tell me about two or three of your favorite music groups. Why do you like them?

Have you seen their videos?

What do they generally sing about?

What do you think their lyrics are saying?

What makes this artist so good?

What are the names of artists that you think I wouldn't approve of?

Why do you think I wouldn't approve of them?

If you could be in a band, what instrument would you play?

Do you like to sing?

7

Still Throwing Up
After All These Years

JENNI'S FRIEND IN ATHENS, GEORGIA, was a great pal—and six
years older than she.

"Hey, why don't you come up and do some barhopping with
me?" said Allison. "I'm turning twenty-one next week."

"Ally, I'm so happy for you, but you know I'm fifteen. I'll
get carded if I try to get into a bar."

"I already thought of that," said Allison. "I just went to the
Department of Motor Vehicles and told them I lost my
license. You can use my old license since the picture is three
years old, and we have the same haircut. It's going to be great!
When you turn twenty-one, bars give you free drinks."

Jenni and Allison had a great time "celebrating" Allison's
twenty-first birthday, if you call barhopping and downing free
liquor the elixir of memories. Jenni is lucky she remembers anything. After drinking half the night away, the two young women
departed the Armadillo Haven, a western honky-tonk joint, for

some fresh air. Jenni was drunk, and her head spun like a dime-store top. She lay down on a park bench, discombobulated. Allison became concerned when Jenni failed to respond to her ministrations. An ambulance was called, and two hours later, ER docs pumped out the bilious contents of Jenni's stomach.

When a woozy Jenni came to, hospital authorities asked her for some identification. She reached into her pants pocket and pulled out her friend's ID—which prompted a phone call to Allison's parents. The phone call wasn't a welcomed one. Fearing a lawsuit, Allison's parents decided not to call Jenni's parents about the incident. They allowed their insurance company to pick up the considerable ER charges and ambulance ride. To this day, Jenni's parents don't know that their daughter nearly died from alcohol poisoning outside the Armadillo Haven.

If you think that drinking has become passé and that throwing up on your shoes is a thing of the past, you should think again. Teen drinking is bigger than ever, and it's starting earlier and earlier.

How do they develop a taste for "adult beverages"? They believe drinking is cool, and alcohol's "coolness" is packaged for them by the mainstream media. Fingers can also be pointed at the advertising industry, since beer companies such as Anheuser-Busch employ talking frogs to push beer sales. "Beer-and-bikini" ads target a youth-oriented audience.

Everywhere teenagers look, they see a society that condones drinking—or gives it a wink of the eye. From wall-to-wall advertising in major sporting events to concert tour sponsorship to "product placement" in PG and PG-13 movies, tipping an ice-cold one is part of the culture. How does James Bond like his martini? Everyone knows: "shaken not stirred."

I've heard it said that once a teen starts drinking regularly, he becomes an alcoholic within eighteen months. Some become alcoholics with the first drink. Teens find it difficult to stop drinking once they develop a taste for alcohol. They are prone to "binge" drinking. *You drink to get drunk, right?*

Not a Good Mix

Let's go over some other reasons why teens and alcohol are not a good mix. Liquor is dangerous, especially when teens are driving and drinking. Every June, millions of American parents hold their breaths on Prom Night. Why? They've read too many newspaper accounts of drunk teens wrapping the family SUV around a power pole or careening into head-on traffic. When teens are drinking, their sense of right and wrong and decision making is diminished. A single beer places most teens over the legal definition of being "impaired": .08 percent alcohol in the bloodstream.

Drinking is also the gateway to smoking pot, which is the gateway to pills, which is the gateway to ecstasy and other hallucinogens. Drinking sets up date rape situations. Long before ecstasy and GHB became popular among the teen masses, guys plied their dates or acquaintances with booze because alcohol lowered their inhibitions. Drunk girls were usually putty in their arms.

While drinking is a gateway drug, many teens view imbibing alcohol as more acceptable than doing drugs. Some kids keep the drug scene at arm's length because they are convinced of its dangers or because they are scared that their parents will find out.

And alcohol is easy to score. Besides raiding their parents' liquor cabinet, teens drink with their friends in the back of cars, on the way to the movies, or at keg parties held at a friend's house. (The parents are *always* gone for the weekend.) Raves and nightclubs gladly sell to underage drinkers.

> I used to go to keg parties at my friend's house. His dad had several empty kegs in his garage, so when his parents were gone for the weekend, my friend had the kegs filled. Many kids who came didn't want to get into drugs, so they thought drinking wasn't as bad. What they didn't know was that drinking is as bad as drugs. You can't drive when you're drunk, and you can't walk very well either. You certainly can't be very intelligent.
>
> —*Sherona*, age fourteen

> I started drinking when I was twelve because I didn't think there was anything wrong with it. I stole stuff from my grandmother's liquor cabinet. I filled bottles with water so she wouldn't think anything was gone.
>
> —*Robbie*, age fifteen

Now that we've established the seriousness of the problem, what are fathers and mothers to do? First, take stock of your personal situation. How much social drinking do you do? Is your idea of a fun Saturday afternoon sipping long-necks at the local sports bar? Do you abuse alcohol?

Drinking actions *scream* louder than words. Most parents—nearly all parents—do not take drugs in front of their children. However, if you're pounding down one Bud after another while screaming at the referee on the TV, slurring your words more with each passing quarter, guess who's taking notes?

Another mistake that parents make is thinking wrong-headedly about alcohol. House of Hope teens have told us their parents made the following statements about drinking:

1. "I don't want you drinking, but if you do, then drink in the house."

Parents think this enlightened approach will make them look cool in their kids' eyes, but it really doesn't. They figure that since their kids will drink anyway, they might as well "control" it by having teens drink under their own roofs.

"My friend's mom bought us wine coolers to drink," said Kerri. "Then Sandra and I drank them with her mom. She always said, 'I'll buy you guys wine coolers as long as you drink at home. As long as you don't go anywhere, that's fine with me.' That gave me the idea that Sandra's mom didn't care. When I got the idea that she didn't care, I figured I could do whatever I wanted, and so did Sandra."

Instead of trying to win a popularity contest, try to win a parenting contest. Good parents set commonsense boundaries, and a commonsense boundary is keeping alcohol out of the hands of minors. If they get used to drinking alcohol inside the home, you will not be able to stop them from drinking outside the home. The world does not operate that way.

2. "Hey, Junior, pick me up a six-pack of Sam Adams."

Several House of Hope teens have told us that they felt like "big dogs" when Dad barked a good-natured command to go over to the supermarket refrigerator case to get his favorite brand of beer. Not a good idea. "It's kind of like opening a door that should be shut in the first place," said Evan.

3. "Does my daughter drink? No way."

This is a head-in-the-sand approach. Consider this interview I did with Marianna:

Sara: What did you drink, Marianna?

Marianna: I drank anything from a beer to hard liquor. I would drink tequila or Crown Royal, or sometimes I drank a Bud Light in the afternoon when my dad wasn't around and I was home by myself.

Sara: Where did you get the booze?

Marianna: My dad was a Bud Light drinker, so he kept it around for family get-togethers. He never noticed when I took one. Either that, or he never said anything. Sometimes I'd get Crown Royal from a friend next door.

Sara: Was your dad fooled every time?

Marianna: Yes.

Sara: When did you start drinking?

Marianna: At the age of fifteen.

Sara: Did this become something you did every weekend?

Marianna: Yes, but I also drank two or three times during the week. Weekends were reserved for partying.

Sara: What did your parents say about your staying out late or coming back home glassy-eyed?

Marianna: They never knew. I stayed a lot at friends' houses. When we went out, we would sneak back into my friend's room late. When I didn't spend the night somewhere else, I would come home late at night and find my mom already asleep. The next morning, she would always ask me where I had been. I would say that a car broke down or give some other lame excuse for my tardiness. But most of the time I would just spend the night with friends so I would have a good excuse to go out partying.

Sara: That's a popular excuse for kids, isn't it?

Marianna: Yes, because it works.

Sara: What are other mistakes that parents make regarding teen drinking?

Marianna: I think the biggest mistake parents make is drinking around teenagers and leaving open beers and liquor bottles around the house. I can remember times when my dad stuck an unfinished can of beer into the refrigerator. It was easy to drink a little bit of that. Plus, I saw a lot of drinking growing up. My grandfather is an alcoholic, so that's where I picked up my desire to drink.

Sara: Did your parents watch sports and drink a lot?

Marianna: No, they weren't into sports. They were into having friends over and hanging out in the pool area and drinking. That told me that drinking was okay and it wasn't a bad thing.

Sara: Did your parents tell you that you had to wait until you were twenty-one to drink?

Marianna: No. My dad always told me that drinking beer was not a big deal as long as you controlled it. I thought drinking could help me escape from what I was feeling. Drinking is what I did when I needed to get over a breakup with a boyfriend, or when I felt alone and depressed.

Sara: Do you remember when you first tried drinking?

Marianna: The first time I ever tasted a beer, I liked it. That's weird because normally kids don't like the taste of beer.

Sara: How old were you?

Marianna: I was probably ten. We were all sitting around the pool on a hot summer's day. I asked my dad, "Can I try a sip of that?" He said, "Sure." He handed me his beer. I tried a sip and actually liked it.

Sara: And everybody laughed, right?

Marianna: Yeah. Everybody thought it was funny. But nobody thought it was funny when I found myself with a big drinking problem five years later.

There you have it, Mom and Dad. One thing I've found out about teens over the years is that if you can help them take an early stand against drinking—or taking drugs or having premarital sex—they will have a better chance of keeping their stand during their teen years. They will have a greater respect for you as parents. Teens are looking for you to be role models, not their best friends.

One way to teach them to say no to drinking is to role-play with your teens. Pretend you are one of your son's (or daughter's) friends:

Dad: Hey, Billy, wanna go drinking?
Son: Nah, I don't think so.
Dad: What's the matter? Are you chicken?
Son: No, I just don't want to.
Dad: You're going to miss out on a lot of fun.
Son: That's okay.
Dad: Everyone will be there.
Son: I don't care. I'll be doing the right thing.

You know the drill, and so do your children. Give them lines that will help them stay away from alcohol, drugs, and sex. Then when they actually get "hit up," they will have the verbal skills to walk away.

Karli was one such person who had those skills. Here's what she said to her friends:

"I want to let you know that I don't drink. I made this decision a long time ago, and I'm not going to do things that I know many of my friends are doing. I still want to have a good time with you, but the only difference is that I won't be drinking with you all. I don't want you to be intimidated by that, but still, I don't want you to think that I'm weird. I just want you to know that not drinking is part of me."

Teens usually respect statements like that. They'll say things like "That's cool," or "To each his own." They may even have friends confide that they wish they weren't sucked into the drinking world.

"Here's what I learned," said Karli. "By taking a stand early with my friends, *I never had to take a stand again.* All along, I was afraid that my friends would resent me or not be friends with me because I was different. But none of that happened. I knew some girls who were party animals—they drank like fish and slept with whomever. They decided they wanted to turn their lives around, but since they had been viewed as party girls from the beginning, it was very difficult for them to change their reputations."

Did you catch what Karli was saying? You can boil her advice down to a single sentence: *You only get one chance to make a first impression.* Tell your teens that they will have a much easier time if they make their stand way in the beginning.

Discussion Starters

Is drinking popular at your school?
What do teens like to drink these days?
What do you think when you see adults drink?
Do I drink too much?
Why is drinking bad for you?
Do you know any teens who've got into car accidents
    because they were drinking?
What happened to them?
Have you been offered a chance to drink?
What did you say?
Do you think you made the right choice?
Should we role-play this situation?

The Guy-Girl Thing

ONE OF THE MOST ASKED QUESTIONS we hear from parents is: *When should I allow my teen to date?*

Before we give you our opinion, we must state up front that we do not allow House of Hope teens to date since they have their hands full learning how to submit to authority figures and overcoming past hurts, disappointments, and bad memories. Taking away the boy-girl pairing-off equation makes life easier for everyone.

We have other reasons for not allowing our adolescents to date. Teens who aren't dating aren't having sex (in the vast majority of cases). Teens who aren't dating travel through adolescence without feeling pressure to be someone's "eye candy" or "boy toy." Teens who aren't dating aren't worrying about sexually transmitted diseases, unwanted pregnancies, or their hearts being broken when the affair breaks up, which happens in more than 99 percent of teen boy-girl relationships.

The House of Hope teens understand that boy-girl interaction of this kind is *verboten* during their stay with us. This
doesn't mean that they can't relate to each other, take classes
together, sit in the same church pew, eat at the same table,
hang out, play basketball, swing dance, sing karaoke, or go on
group outings together. In fact, we encourage all those things.
What we promote at the House of Hope is the feeling that
when boys and girls are doing an activity (say, going to the
McCormacks for an afternoon of boating and swimming),
they do it in a group setting, much like a group date.

Group dating, I can assure you, is the way to go. It's a concept you should carefully consider for your teens. By group
dating, we mean two, three, four or more guys getting together
with two, three, four or more girls for a fun activity—and no
pairing off. Group dating is a fabulous way for teens to get to
know the opposite sex without all the baggage that comes from
who-is-doing-what-with-so-and-so.

Protect More Than Their Hearts

After working with teens for more than thirty years, I would
be very careful about granting adolescents the freedom—or
responsibility—to single date or even double date before they
are seventeen years old. The concept that you want to get
across to your teens in the early adolescent years is the concept of getting to know the opposite sex in group settings.
When they ask why (and they will), reply that you want to
protect them from sexual mischief.

Teens generally do not have the emotional maturity to successfully handle a boy-girl relationship. On top of that, boys
and girls arrive at different maturity levels at different times,
which causes a mismatch since girls generally mature earlier

than their male counterparts. This is why you'll see fifteen-year-old girls attracted to college-age guys; the little twerps in her class are just a bunch of immature brats in her mind. What she doesn't realize is that she lacks the emotional maturity to rebuff a nineteen-year-old male's sexual advances.

There's another thing you should know about the teen-dating scene. America's teenagers don't travel to "Lover's Lane" anymore with the idea of having sex in the back seat of the car. No, they're having sex in the comfort of their own homes, usually between the hours of 3 P.M. and 5 P.M. before Mom gets home from work. The boyfriend goes over to the girlfriend's house (or vice versa) after the final school bell rings. With their hormones on fire and no parent on duty (and their siblings engrossed by TV or homework), they end up "experimenting" in bed.

A study by *Public Health Reports* shows that young boys whose mothers are employed full-time have rates of sexual experience 45 percent higher than those of male classmates whose nonemployed mothers are home when they arrive home from school. Another study, done by the *Journal of Marriage and the Family*, reports similar findings for young girls. This "four o'clock sex" underscores the need for flexible work arrangements so that by working at home, working part-time, or reorganizing their work schedules, mothers can be home when their children are not in school.

So What's a Parent to Do?

I very much like the advice that Sandra P. Aldrich, a speaker and former public-school teacher in Michigan, shares when she talks to audiences about the guy-girl thing. Sandra stresses three points that parents should keep in mind:

1. Expect your teen to have high standards. Maybe it's a sign of the times, but many parents *expect* their sons and daughters to be sexually active with their dates. They'll say things like "We know that boys will be boys" or "Be sure that your feelings don't run away with you," which convey the ideas that teen sex is inevitable or that sexual feelings are so strong that they can overrule judgment. Those are incorrect messages to send, as is the practice of quietly slipping condoms into purses.

At the House of Hope, we expect our teens to set very high standards for themselves. Besides dating being off limits, they cannot engage in any intimate physical contact. Our words and our actions let them know that *real* young men and *real* young women act responsibly. We remind them that sexual feelings don't have to be acted upon any more than feelings of anger. Another thing we say is, "You may not be able to control your feelings, but you *can* control your actions."

2. Express trust in your teen. If you go around the house accusing your daughter of being a tramp or your son of being worse than a sex-happy Al Bundy (the "dad" on the *Married . . . With Children* TV show), they will live up to those low expectations. You're not raising the bar very high. Let them know that you're confident they will make the right choice regarding whom they date and where the relationship will go.

3. When your teen is allowed to date, get to know that person beforehand. Sandra Aldrich became a single parent while her two children were still in elementary school. When Holly reached high school, a bevy of boys lined up to ask her out. This prompted Sandra to start a little routine known as The Talk.

The Talk consists of having Holly's would-be date knock on the front door and being welcomed into the home by Sandra. Holly is nowhere to be seen. Meanwhile, Sandra seats the young man on the family couch and asks a series of pleasant questions, starting with "How long have you lived in this area?" and "Do you have brothers and sisters?" Within a few minutes, the questions advance to "What are you planning to study in college?" and "What church does your family attend?"

Invariably, the young man answers the questions in a typical teen monotone while continually looking toward the stairway, wondering when Holly will be ready.

"It's okay," smiles Sandra. "She'll be downstairs when this is over."

Things are getting serious now.

Sandra settles herself into the sofa corner. "I didn't know anything about you before this chat," she says. "Right now, you think this is ridiculous, but I guarantee you that in about twenty-five years when a guy asks your future daughter out, you'll think of me and say, 'That old lady was right!'"

Sandra lets that thought sink in before continuing. "I know you two are just going out as friends, but I've lived long enough to know how quickly situations can change. So remember this: Treat Holly the way you hope some other guy is treating your future wife tonight."

The boy's eyes widen at the thought. Sandra knows that she's hit her target.

If you choose to incorporate The Talk in your home, then you can figure that word of your little tête-à-tête will get around school. But look at this development as a plus. If some gum-smacking teen boy doesn't want to meet you beforehand, preferring to lean on the horn in the driveway, then he's someone who isn't good dating material for your daughter anyway—the child you love above everything on earth. Let him keep beeping his horn, or better yet, walk out to the car and tell him the date is off.

I would also counsel parents to get to know their son's date. Perhaps after he picks her up, he can drive her back to the house for a "Hi, how are you" get together. Sure, such interactions can be awkward; as parents, we may not get through this stage as well as we'd like, but talking to our children about our dating expectations and being ever watchful of who they go out with increases our chances of raising them to make good moral choices.

Isn't that the goal of every parent? Of course it is. Now I'm going to turn the rest of this chapter over to Karen Buck, one of our House of Hope counselors, who has a great personal story of how she handled teen dating in her household.

Karen Buck's Story

Our family has seen all the teenybopper movies that try to paint the picture that if teenagers don't have a boyfriend or girlfriend by eleven or twelve years of age, they are out of it. Schools play into this mindset by sponsoring dances for sixth grade kids. The Associated Student Body board won't say that you need a date to attend a dance, but the kids pick up on the importance of pairing up. This causes the parents to think, *Well, if they can go to a little school dance together, why not let them see a movie together or go out for a pizza?*

The result: you have twelve-year-old kids who are dating, almost by default. Peer pressure only exacerbates the issue, causing preadolescents to whine, "Mom, if you don't let me go to the movie with Alec, I'm going to be a social failure."

What happens is that parents get adjusted to Missy going to the mall to see a movie with Alec before they finish middle school. This is where moms and dads need to stop and think through what kinds of rules or guidelines they will have about dating. I think it's important to give your children some freedom and let them do some things, but you also want some rules to preserve certain teen rites of passage for their junior and senior years.

For instance, if my children had started going to dances in the sixth grade, then the junior dance in high school would have been boring. They would have had to get drunk or sneak out and make out in the back seat of somebody's car to have fun. I didn't want them to reach prom night with a "been there, done that" attitude. Guess what? For our kids, the senior prom was a wonderful evening that my children haven't forgotten.

Let me amplify this point. My husband and I raised four teenagers who have become successful young adults. What we tried to instill in our four children was the idea of saving something for later; don't embark on every pleasure of life the very first moment you have a chance to do so. They understood this regarding dating. With each year of age, they received another dating privilege. Here's what we said to our teens:

- Prior to age fifteen, you can have friends over to the house, or you can go over to your friends' homes, if we know the parents.
- At age fifteen, you can group date.
- At age sixteen, you can group date.
- At age seventeen, you can go on single dates.
- At age eighteen, you can make your own schedule, and you don't have to clear it with us. You are young adults.

Our dating rules were more liberal than what we teach parents at the House of Hope. If my husband and I had to do it over again, our teens would have group dated until their senior year of high school—that's how much we believe in this approach. We promote group dating in our counseling situations with fathers and mothers at the House of Hope.

Our children certainly did things in group settings for most of their adolescence. When each child turned thirteen or fourteen, I said they could invite all their friends to come over to our house. If one of those friends happened to be somebody that they liked to hold hands with, fine. Our house became a place where my kids and their friends liked to congregate. Sure, our grocery bill went through the roof, but this also gave us the advantage of knowing who their friends were and what activities they were doing. We figured buying pizza ingredients, soft drinks, and ice cream by the vanload was cheaper than putting them in a twelve-step program five years later.

We gave the kids their space. My husband and I frequently took books and read in our bedroom, or we stayed in the kitchen constructing homemade pizzas while the kids had fun in the living room watching videos, playing games, or just talking while they wolfed down finger foods. I found that when I brought a pan of piping hot pizza or a tray of fresh chocolate chip cookies to the family room, some of the kids would follow me back to the kitchen because they wanted to talk about what was on their minds.

When our children asked whether they could go over to a friend's house on a Friday night, we approved if we knew the parents. If we didn't, then I told the kids that I had to talk to the mom. I wanted to ask two questions: Will there be adult supervision? Will there be alcohol served?

I will admit that the latter question startled a few parents, but I didn't care. I was more interested in the welfare of my children than the peer pressure of attending a you-gotta-be-there party. I had parents who said, "No, we're not going to be home," and when I heard that, I said, "Thank you very much, but our children won't be coming."

That only happened a couple of times before our children wised up. They stopped asking when they knew a party was being thrown because the parents were going to be out of town.

When the children turned fifteen years of age, we gave them more privileges. We said they could start going places with a group of friends. Again, if one had a boyfriend or girl-friend in that group, that was fine. They could all go to a bas-ketball or football game together. We didn't mind driving them since they were prelicense age. If they wanted to go out for pizza or somewhere afterward, that was also fine. We never had a set time that they had to be home because the cur-few was always determined by what time the activity ended. For instance, if the football game finished at 9:30 P.M., we did not allow a 1 A.M. curfew since three-and-a-half hours was a long time to figure out what to do. If a concert or youth event ended at 11 P.M., however, we always said it was fine to stay out another hour getting an ice cream. We just had to know.

One of the things we did was tell the kids that from time to time we would check on them—but never embarrass them. I remember walking into Pizza Hut and "yoo-hooing" from the entrance, but I didn't interrupt their good time. On each occasion when they were where they were supposed to be, trust built up between us.

One time, we had a daughter in her junior year of high school dating a boy named Rob who was a freshman in college. One evening, Rob decided to come home from school early for a long weekend break. I had promised to take the three younger kids out to a movie, and my husband was out of town. My daughter Beth suddenly said, "Mom, I don't think I want to go to the movies." How dumb did she think I was?

"Honey," I said, "you know Dad's not here, and you can't have anybody over when I'm not here."

Beth nodded. She knew our standards.

I didn't force her to go to the movie with us because she's a great kid, and she had never given us a reason *not* to trust her. I took the other children, and once they were settled in the movie, I slipped out into the lobby and phoned the boy's house to see whether he was home. His mother answered.

"No, Rob's not here," she said.

My heart sank. I really didn't want them to be up to anything.

"Oh, do you know where he is?"

"Rob's over at church, helping my husband paint the fellowship hall."

Not only is the kid not doing something wrong, I thought, *but he's a saint!*

"Karen, can I ask why you're calling?"

"Libby, it's nothing. Never mind. I'll talk to you later."

On the way home I was thinking that Libby would tell Rob about my prying phone call, and Rob would surely tell my daughter. Sure enough, when we got home from the movies, Beth was livid.

"Mom, did you call and check up on me?" she demanded.

For a brief moment, I thought about telling a white lie—that I was trying to plan a surprise party for her. Then I told myself, *Karen, nothing works like the truth.*

"Yes, honey, I did."

"I can't believe you checked up on me!"

"I know, and I know what kind of a girl you are. Ninety-eight percent of the time I can trust you to do the right thing. But there's that little 2 percent of the time when the temptation to do what you want to do comes to the forefront. It's my job as your parent to help you through that 2 percent of the time. I'm telling this from my own personal experience, and it's this: no one is 100 percent trustworthy. That's why God gave parents to their kids, to help them get through the rough things until they're adults."

When Beth kissed me good night, she said, "I can't believe you did that, but I'm not angry with you."

"Why's that?"

"Because you caught me doing the right thing."

That was a wonderful teaching opportunity with my daughter, a bonding moment between us that showed her how much I loved her and how much I expected of her and what she was capable of.

You can give your teenagers the same feeling of responsibility by providing leadership and wheelbarrows of love in the home.

Discussion Starters

What is dating?
Do you have friends who date?
What do they do?
What makes a date fun?
Do you know what group dating is?
What are the advantages of group dating?
What are the disadvantages of group dating?
What do you think of having us meet your date before you go out?

9

Going All the Way

At the House of Hope, we realize that the concept of teen dating seems like a dreamy anachronism to today's teens, a reminder of a bygone era when kids cruised Main Street in their hot rods and stopped at the malt shoppe to sip a single chocolate shake with double straws.

These days, many teens dispense with the preliminaries—dating, going steady, getting "pinned"—and cut straight to the chase. They "get down"—engage in sexual intercourse—within days, hours, even minutes after being attracted to each other. Some couples even go to the trouble of learning each other's first name.

Not many boys or girls under the age of sixteen arrive at the House of Hope with their virginity intact. On the male side, there was nothing holding them back, so they went for it. Why not? It sure felt good. Why should the adults have all the fun?

As for the girls, some gave their virginity away before leaving elementary school. They lacked the maturity to understand what they were doing, although they hoped that by giving sex they would receive love.

It didn't happen.

Other girls felt pressured not to be "left behind" in the middle-school years; there were boys willing to accommodate them. A smaller percentage of girls held out until high school, but eventually they let their hormones and peer pressure get the best of them. Then there are the teen girls whose sexual innocence was brutally stolen from them. They were raped by gang members, sexually used by ravers who spiked their drinks, or were forced into performing various sexual acts by stepparents or their mother's boyfriends or trusted family relatives. A small percentage sold their bodies to buy drugs. For these teens, the idea of "hooking up" with Joe Quarterback at Lover's Lane sounds like a passage from a Harlequin romance novel.

The issue of teenage sexuality is an important one because early sexual activity usually changes the course of a teen's life—especially for young women. They are the ones left holding the six-pound "bundle of joy" long after the father has split. They are the ones crying themselves to sleep in the weeks, months, and even years following an abortion. They are the ones experiencing painful sexually transmitted diseases such as chlamydia and HPV, or human papillomavirus, which has been linked to more than 90 percent of invasive cervical cancers. They are the ones feeling empty and hollow when the relationship is over. When teens start having sex, pretty soon that's all they have in common. They certainly can't go back to kissing because physical intimacy is progressive.

This is not to exonerate the male since it takes two to tango. He got what he wanted, but society doesn't compel him to take any responsibility or experience any shame. Our culture is saying *love the one you're with*. The concept of "free love" that captivated the Woodstock generation has turned out to be free for him and not so free for her.

Back in Control

When kids enter the House of Hope, they quickly learn where we stand on the issue of premarital sex. We promote abstinence and teach that "safe sex" really isn't very safe. Even condoms are only 90 percent effective and not nearly as efficient as everyone makes them out to be. And when you have inexperienced teens, in the heat of the moment, trying to make sure it's on right, the failure rate is even worse!

A. C. Green, a veteran NBA star with the Miami Heat, owns two impressive streaks for a professional basketball player: one is the all-time record for the most consecutive games (more than 1,100) and the other is remaining a virgin all his life. A. C., a bachelor, has this to say about teaching "safe sex" to our kids: "It's a lie to say that putting on a condom makes you as secure as Fort Knox. I cringe when I hear that stuff. Condoms have a hard enough time just stopping a woman from getting pregnant, let alone blocking an HIV virus, which is 450 times smaller than sperm itself. It's like water going through a net."

Simultaneously, we recognize that there are teens who jump the gun and need a loving arm around the shoulder plus a measure of grace. With those teens, we trumpet a concept called "recycled virginity." Teens who have fallen short can recommit themselves to staying out of bed until their wedding nights. We tell them they are back in control of their bodies. Frequently, teen rebellion and hell-raising are all about who's in control. Well, here's something they can control—their bodies.

> I was sexually involved with more than a dozen guys before I came to the House of Hope. Now I'm a secondary virgin for lots reasons. No one my age is really emotionally ready for sex. I would tell any teen girls thinking about getting involved sexually that guys will get what they want, but you'll never have a real relationship with them. When I was in the middle of my affairs, I didn't think that, but when I stepped back and took an objective look, I realized that I was just being used. Since vowing to stay sexually pure until I marry, I feel really good about myself.
>
> —*Magdalena*, fifteen years of age

Listen to this exchange between Karen Buck, one of our counselors, and a teen girl new to the program:

Karen: Keri, God gave you a wonderful body and made you special. Now you have an opportunity to be a virgin again. You can become a recycled virgin and start all over again. It's your choice as a teenager. You have that control.

Keri: I don't think so.

Karen: Oh, but you do. We will help give you the ability to make the right choices. You have the choice to never let anyone use your body in an imperfect way. You can set boundaries.

Before you came to the House of Hope, I counseled a girl who confessed to me that she had been having sex with her sixteen-year-old boyfriend. I asked her, "What are your needs? What are you looking for? What did he need in a girlfriend?"

I helped her to see that they both wanted something different. She learned that she was willing to sacrifice her virginity for being held and kissed and told that she was pretty. He was not willing to sacrifice anything for her, which she saw for the first time. Everything had to be done on his timetable. I told her that I wasn't saying he wasn't a nice guy, or that he was the most selfish person who ever walked the planet, but he was looking out for Number One—himself.

Keri: Aren't boys *always* looking out for themselves?

Karen: Let's talk about commitment for a moment. It's kind of like the old story about the pig and the chicken. It seems that one day a pig and a chicken were walking down the street, and the chicken sees that a poor family doesn't have anything to eat.

"We could give them breakfast," said the chicken.

The pig says to the chicken, "Easy for you to say. It won't cost you very much, but it'll cost me everything." That is an excellent picture of the cost of sex to teenagers. Sex will cost the girl everything she's got, and she'll never be quite the same. The same does not hold true for males. Sex will cost him very little. However, when two people become one during sex, they give a little bit of themselves in physical, emotional, and spiritual ways.

Keri, there are times that you will feel that you *need* sex. It's natural to think that way, but sex is not a basic need. Love and acceptance by friends and family are basic needs. Security is a basic need. So is breathing and eating. Having sex with your boyfriend, however, is not essential to your life.

Keri: But can I really wait? It seems impossible. What did your children do?

Karen: From the time my oldest daughter Beth was eight or nine years old, I promised her that I would answer any question she asked about sex, no matter how personal or how embarrassing it might be. I did this because I didn't want Beth to learn about sex the way I did, which left me feeling that intercourse was ugly, filthy, and not at all enjoyable. It took a long time for me and my tender, gentle husband, to overcome my low sexual desire, which was based on what I heard growing up about sex.

Beth put me to the test when she was ten years old.

"Mom, what are wet dreams?"

I nearly choked on my coffee.

I remembered my promise, so I plunged ahead. We talked about wet dreams in age-appropriate terms. When I finished, I looked at her.

"Oh, I thought it had something to do with wetting your bed. I wet my bed last night."

So that's what she meant by wet dreams!

I chuckled, but I knew I had done the right thing. To say something like "Where did you hear that?" or "Who have you been talking to?" would have meant that was the *last* time my daughter would innocently approach me with a question about sex.

As my four children grew up, they heard me talk about the importance of staying sexually pure, how everyone was *not* doing it. I reminded each of our daughters that the greatest gift she could give her husband on their wedding night would be a sexually pure body. Then we reiterated that no question about sex was too personal and that they could talk about anything.

That approach served my husband, Bob, and me well. I remember when our daughter Kathy came home during her freshman year of college. We started talking, and Kathy told me about a boy she liked.

"We were putting some stuff away in a closet after class, and he turned around and kissed me," said Kathy.

"Oh, really," I said, not wanting to rush the story. I knew Kathy well enough to know that she had not been kissed very often.

"Then he started to pull down the zipper on my shirt. I said, 'Wait a minute. What do you think you're doing?'"

My other daughter, Beth, was listening to this conversation. She noticed how I kept my cool as I asked a few questions—not in an accusatory tone—that caused Kathy to think.

"What did you think when this happened?"

"What do you think this tells you about the boy?"

"Does this tell you anything about the kind of person he is?"

Mostly I drew answers out of her. I never said "Don't do that again" or "You must have done something to encourage him." I knew that at her age she would do whatever she chose to do. She had to make her own standards at this point.

When Beth reached her senior year of college, she was a resident assistant—RA—in the dorms. A wonderful young man asked her to marry him, and she accepted. All the girls on Beth's floor—around twenty-eight—congregated in her room, giggling like schoolgirls. They wanted to know about her mysterious boyfriend, what he was like—the lowdown.

One young woman asked Beth, "How long before you get married are you supposed to stop having sex?"

"What?" asked Beth.

"You know. When do you stop so that it will be fun on your wedding night? You know. Make it more special."

"Well, what makes sex special is never to start," replied Beth.

"Never to start? Are you saying..."

"What I'm saying is the greatest gift you can give your husband is the fact that you've saved yourself for him."

"You're kidding, aren't you?" asked one freshman.

"You mean you've never been with a man?" chimed in another.

"That's right," replied Beth matter-of-factly. She heard one girl whisper, "What planet does she live on?" but she pretended not to hear. Beth had a reputation for being really cool. She lived close to the edge and knew how to have fun, but she also had a strong set of standards. Beth knew what was important.

Several months later, Beth walked down the aisle on her father's arm and pledged to love Joe in sickness and health, to have and to hold, until death did them part. After the wedding reception, they took our car to stay at an airport hotel on their wedding night before flying to the Caribbean the next morning.

The plan was for us to retrieve our car at the airport the following morning. When I opened the car door, I saw a yellow Post-It note sticking to the dashboard. On it were two words: "Wow, Mom!"

Keri: That's what I have to say, too—Wow! Thanks for telling me that story. But what do you say to the boys? It seems like girls always have to be the ones to say no.

Karen: I would tell boys that when they have sex with a girl, then they're hurting this girl in a permanent, psychological kind of way. If he really loved her, he wouldn't want to do that to her. As a matter of fact, I would remind him that it's a natural role for males to want to protect her and provide for her.

Keri: And their urges?

Karen: I would remind them that I know that they have these natural urges, but they are not urges that they can't live without. Boys will survive just fine by postponing sex. As a matter of fact, it would be healthier for them to wait until it's the right time—like right after a wedding. Waiting can protect the mind from sexual comparisons. Guys frequently compare the sexual performance of one female against another, or compare her body to others that he has seen naked. He replays these scenes in his mind, which can't be good for a relationship that the two of you want to last for a lifetime.

A couple that waits for one another builds up *trust* in each other. They know—unless they've jumped the gun—that their partner will not bring a sexually transmitted disease to the marriage bed. As of right now, there are more than three dozen STDs that can render couples sterile, cause cancer, or shorten their life span.

You will feel great pressure throughout your teen years to engage in premarital sex. Society's attitude of "Well, they're going to do it anyway" pushes millions of teenagers into a world of promiscuity—many who would have waited, if they had only been encouraged to do so. Believe me, it's worth it to save sex for marriage, for the partner you've pledged to spend the rest of your life with. Don't do it! The rest of your life is ahead of you, and it's worth fighting for. Once you do find that special person, you'll never regret your decision to postpone sexual activity.

Discussion Starters

Questions to ask if you think your teen has not been
   sexually active:

Why do you think sex is so hard for parents and teens
   to talk about?
Have we talked too little or too much about teen sexu-
   ality in the past?
Do you know how I feel about premarital sex?
Why do you think it's important to wait?
Are there any questions you want to ask me about sex?
Do you think you are well versed on sex?
What have they taught you in school about sex?
Would you say more than half or less than half of the
   boys and girls in your school are virgins?
Has any boy (or girl) put pressure on you to have sex?
How did you feel about that?

Questions to ask if you think your teen has been sexually active:

Why do you think sex is so hard for parents and teens
   to talk about?
Have we talked too little or too much about teen sexu-
   ality in the past?
Do you know how I feel about premarital sex?
Why do you think it's important to wait?
Are there any questions you want to ask me about sex?
Have you ever heard of the concept "recycled virginity"?
What do you think it means?
What do you think the benefits are of not having sex?
Would you like to become a secondary virgin?

10

Hanging Out with Their Set

ADAM WAS ONLY SIXTEEN YEARS OLD, but he was given a man's job: drive over to a crack house to buy two kilos of cocaine. His gang boss handed Adam $6,000 in cash, which the teen stuffed into his jacket. Then he hopped in a car for a short drive.

Adam followed directions well. He knocked on the door of the ramshackle house. The door cracked open an inch and then swung open. They were expecting him.

"I'm here to pick up a couple of keys," said Adam, hoping that his voice wouldn't crack from the nervousness he felt in his throat.

The drug dealer, who looked to be in his early twenties, jerked his head toward the living room. "You can sit on the couch," he said. Adam dropped his bulky frame onto the tattered sofa and took a deep breath. When he looked up, he felt the cold muzzle of a .22 caliber barrel pressed against his forehead—right between his eyes. A furtive glance revealed that two guys holding semiautomatic weapons flanked the dude with the gun.

"The money. Give me the money."

That's when Adam realized that he wasn't leaving the crack house with the delivery. Then he wondered if he would be leaving the house alive. *Act cool,* he told himself. *This happens all the time.*

Adam decided his best chance was to hand over the wad of $20s and walk out of the house as nonchalantly as possible. He reached into his jacket, handed over the cash, and walked out as if nothing were amiss. He didn't ask permission; he didn't say a thing. With each step, however, he wondered if it would be his last. The nervous teen finally took a breath when he reached the sidewalk. He started up the car and drove back to his gang leader.

Adam was surprised that his friend didn't fly through the roof when he learned that they had been ripped off to the tune of $6,000.

"Don't worry about it," he said as the gang boss slapped his shoulder. "I'll handle it."

When Adam told me his story, I asked him whether he ever found out what happened to those guys in the crack house.

"I knew better than to ask what happened," said Adam. "I did hear that the boss sent eight men over to the house, and the $6,000 was recovered. My guess is that those three guys are swimming with the fishes."

Bursting the Stereotype

If you do a word association with "gangs," most parents conjure up images of young black males wearing red kerchiefs around their heads, selling "dime bags" of heroin on gritty street corners.

Let me debunk that stereotype. Gang members come in all colors, reach into middle-class neighborhoods, and are equal-opportunity employers. Sure, they sell drugs, but they are also involved in grand theft, fencing goods, and protection rackets. They have no compunction about killing someone standing in their way. Gangs instill fear and intimidate rivals and citizens alike. They routinely extort "protection" money from neighborhood businesses and find violence glamorous and necessary to maintain their "turf." They spraypaint graffiti to "mark" their territory, and certain articles of clothing and colors are strong identifiers. An innocent teen can get shot for walking through a neighborhood wearing the wrong color.

Nationally, blacks and Hispanics constitute the largest number of gang members, followed by white gangs comprised of angry punk rockers and heavy metalers prone to violence. Although most of the teens who've come to the House of Hope over the years have been white, I would say that more than half belonged to a gang. We've even had a few girls peripherally involved with gangs. One "auxiliary member" named Chanda tells her story:

When I was fifteen years old, I dated the leader of one of Orlando's biggest gangs—the Crips. He was twenty years old and black: I was white. If you date the leader, you become part of the gang. They didn't make me go through initiation, but any guy who wanted to join had to go through initiation. The usual initiation was to drive into a mall parking lot in the middle of the day, find a woman, and rape her in broad daylight. Gangs are into sexual power and being strong.

My boyfriend lived in a house with nine other people. His main job was managing cocaine and crack sales, which landed him in jail once. Going to jail is a macho thing for gang members; they act like big dogs when they get out. Another thing they did to earn money was to drive into rich neighborhoods where BMWs and Lexuses were parked in driveways. They would quickly set up the expensive cars on bricks and spin off the tires, making tons of money selling stolen tires to used tire stores. Sometimes they would steal cars and strip them for their parts, which they sold to auto repair shops or junkyards. I even saw gang members stealing boxed-up TVs from the loading dock at Circuit City. They were just *brazen*. Police are generally afraid of gangs because they know gang members kill for no reason.

I would say around 30 percent of kids in lower-income high schools are gang members. In upper middle-class districts, probably 10 percent are involved. Then there are the "wannabes"—rebellious kids who want to be adopted by the brotherhood, but they can never get accepted. I've seen them hang out at gang members' houses, talking about the differences in this type of coke versus that type of coke, thinking they're cool. But they'll always be "wannabes." They aren't cool enough.

The wannabe white kids from the suburbs are captivated by gangs through MTV videos. Some of the popular rappers— Puffy Combs, Dat Nigga Daz, and Kurupt Tha Kingpin, of Tha Dogg Pound—are quasi-gang members anyway, and their "gangsta" rap music glorifies street life while expressing a desire to kill people standing in the way—like cops. That sounds cool to wannabes, who buy into the video image.

> White kids look at those videos of black rap artists and try to copy what they're seeing. They see something alluring in them.
>
> —*Frank*, a House of Hope counselor

Why do young men turn to gangs? Sociologists and police "community service" officers have studied this question for decades. They know that gangs date back to London in the 1600s, when marauding bands of disruptive youths roamed the city. One of the first reports of gangs in this country was in 1791 when city fathers in Philadelphia convened a conference to discuss how to deal with a burgeoning gang problem.

Authorities generally agree that teen boys turn to gangs because they lack a father figure in the home. Reggie Walton, a Superior Court judge in Washington, D.C., blames his heavy caseload of youth-related crime on the disappearance of fathers. Judge Walton told the *Washington Post* that fathers leave children to be raised by young mothers who themselves are often struggling with mental or emotional problems, limited education, poverty, and addiction.

The hotbed for gang recruitment is a household headed by a single-parent mom. I'm sorry to state this so bluntly, but testosterone-heavy teen boys are searching for acceptance, for being accepted for who they are, and—in an upside-down kind of way—unconditional love. They believe their gang can give that to them.

Just because you live in a cul-de-sac with neat lawns and elegant homes doesn't mean that your son (or daughter) couldn't get caught up with some gang-like group. "I don't care where you live," said Kristin. "There are gangs everywhere. There are gangs in the small towns outside Orlando, even living on farms. They are a bunch of kids who want to be loved by someone."

Two rival gangs, the Bloods and the Crips, have a presence in fifty-eight cities in thirty-five states across the country. Three factors can be attributed to the spread of gangs:

1. Parents living in a gang-ravaged community, hoping to protect their adolescent teens from the hometown gang's influence, send their offspring to live with relatives in faraway cities. Sometimes this strategy works, but other times sending young, rebellious youths out of state merely exports gang members to virgin turf.

2. The search for new markets has prompted the Bloods and the Crips to "franchise" their drug-selling gangs in major metropolitan areas around the country.

3. The music and entertainment industries promote the gang culture through movies, rap music, and even comic books. Carefully crafted MTV videos make the gang lifestyle look alluring, which influences favorable press coverage.

But the entertainment media glosses over a few things. Police authorities have noticed that youth violence has escalated dramatically in the last decade as more and more guns fall into the hands of adolescents. Police logs everywhere are awash with drive-by shootings, gangland killings, intergang warfare, and robberies and carjackings at gunpoint. According to the FBI, the fastest growing murder statistic is juvenile gang killings.

Joining a Set

One of our counselors, Frank, came off the streets of New York himself. Frank is an African-American.

> When I was growing up, we called them crews or a posse; these are my boys. You could say, "This is my gang," or "This is my set." When you get right down to it, gangs are all about relationships. For instance, when I was growing up, we were actually racists, probably because of ignorance. We'd be constantly talking about what the white man was up to and what we could do to stop being suppressed. How could we get ahead?

"Living in the ghetto," said Frank, "means living with nothing but negativity: how bad things are, how whitey is out to get you, how the police want to stamp you out like vermin. If you grow up in the suburbs, chances are good that you will have some success. Life is good. Your parents work, there's food on the table; there's something there. You know your relatives. Your grandmother is not forty years old. But in the ghetto, you're hearing the negatives, so you just try to find a way that will make you successful. That was my goal. I wanted to be a successful drug dealer." Frank wanted to be a success at *something*, which is a universal yearning.

There's another reason why young males are drawn to gangs like moths to a flame: money. Gang members selling drugs and fencing stolen goods sweep in thousands of dollars—untaxed—with very little "overhead." Those in the neighborhood trying to stay out of gangs are ridiculed by their peers as "hamburger flippers" earning "chump change" at fast-food joints. Would you rather make $100,000 a year or $10,000 a year? Who can live on the latter amount, even in the inner city?

Author James Q. Wilson, writing in *The Moral Sense*, understands how young males can be drawn to the gang lifestyle. Modern society, he writes, with its "rapid technological change, intense division of labor, and ambiguous allocation of social roles, frequently leaves men out, with their aggressive predispositions either uncontrolled or undirected. Gangs are one result."

> I was involved with a gang, but we didn't like to call ourselves part of a gang. We just liked to hang out, loiter, get in trouble. One time, my crew decided to fight another crew before school. I had a knife. A couple of my friends had mace and chains. Some had guns, but I didn't know who they were. About twenty or thirty kids on each side started fistfighting in the parking lot before the school called the cops.
>
> —*Leon*, age sixteen

I doubt that many parents reading this book are having a problem with their teens belonging—heart, soul, and mind—to a gang. My purpose in including this chapter is to educate you about the pervasiveness of gangs. They have a foothold in many communities, and although they are not large in numbers, they are recruiting.

A son or daughter involved with a gang, however, is a strong signal that the family unit has fractured. I'm also worried about teens attracted to "sets" of friends who operate as a quasi-gang. A set of males hanging out together may not be interested in dealing drugs or taking on the big dogs in the 'hood, yet they could get caught up in a crossfire and find themselves in the wrong place at the wrong time.

> My neighborhood doesn't look like a poor section of town, but it is. There are two major gangs in my area—the Crips and the Bloods. A kid named Moses is the gang leader of the Bloods. Everyone knows Moses as the "big dog" in town. You don't mess with Moses. If Moses wants something, you give it to him.
>
> —*Amanda*, age sixteen

It shouldn't be that difficult to keep your children from joining gangs. If you are meeting your teens' friends, involved in their free time, setting limits on where they can go, being an informed parent should head off any gang-related happenings in your home.

Discussion Starters

Are there any gangs at school?

Are there any gangs in our neighborhood?

Do you know of any gangs, period?

What do gangs do?

Have you ever met a gang member?

What do they dress like?

What would you do if a gang asked you to join?

What do you have to do to get initiated?

What happens to most gang members after a few years?

Are there any gang members in their thirties or forties?

Why is that?

Why are gangs dangerous?

11

Dying to Be Thin

IF I HAD TO GUESS, I would say that half of the girls arrive at
the House of Hope's doorsteps with an eating disorder. It's
that prevalent.

At first glance, we can't tell whether our teen girls are
anorexic or bulimic, but they give us hints in the first week or
two. We notice that they always raise the subject of food and
have an unbelievable focus about the subject. They ask us
questions like: What kind of meals do you have here? Are
there snacks? Are the apples organic or regular? Is this yogurt
low fat or nonfat? How many fat grams in the lasagna? Do
you know how many calories this cake has?

We are fortunate that the House of Hope teens eat well,
thanks to donations from a local supermarket chain. I remember the early days when lunches consisted of PB&J sand-
wiches and the dinner staple was spaghetti with Ragu
sauce—and we were thankful that we had enough to eat!

Today, we serve well-balanced meals with variety, so when a House of Hope teen begins skipping breakfast, picking at her lunch, doing strange things at dinnertime (like pouring ketchup over her salad), acting fearful around fatty foods, reading salad dressing bottle labels, wishing everything we served were low fat or nonfat, we take notes. When they make a big deal about drinking a Diet Coke or always having something in their mouths like sugar-free gum or sugar-free candy—something to keep their mouths moving—then we know they have a fixation with food.

> Sheila was scared of food. She told me that she binged when her family vacationed at the beach. She ate everything she could for four days—she really pigged out. Then she would throw up for three days by drinking water and tickling the back of her throat. Just to be sure she got everything out, she took laxatives.
>
> —*Alicia*, age fifteen

Sheila was what *Zest* magazine calls a "hedged hedonist"— someone willing to do something unhealthy but who compensates for it afterwards. We've heard stories about girls buying a half-gallon of chocolate chip ice cream and trying to eat it in one night. Then they would do a hundred push-ups and a hundred sit-ups and drink a gallon of water, believing everything would cancel out.

This extreme behavior is one reason why eating disorders are a touchy subject. Raising the "ED" issue with teen girls risks sending them underground. Why? If you ask them point-blank if they have an eating disorder, they'll deny it. Those who have been borderline anorexic upon arrival at the

House of Hope often move into bulimic eat-and-purge activity. They do this despite living in a group home situation, where their peers can hear them vomiting in the bathroom. But this still doesn't stop girls from trying, because they are determined to *control* food.

Eating disorders are common, dangerous, and difficult to deal with. Those with eating disorders are enigmas wrapped in loose-fitting clothes. The question of *why* girls (95 percent of eating disorders involve girls and young women) think they're fat, weigh too much, are depressed about their looks, fuss over fat grams, and obsess about miniscule weight gains is difficult to answer.

It's my belief that teen girls are heavily influenced by what they see in fashion magazines. "Runway" magazines such as *Vogue* and *Elle* drip with glamour; models must be rail thin, or they are banished from the *haute couture* of Milan and Paris. (The average model weighs 23 percent less than the average woman.) Teen-targeted publications such as *Seventeen* contain articles on taking laxatives for weight loss or step-by-step directions to following the latest fad diet. Reading these magazines puts ideas in a girl's head.

No wonder a significant survey of female attitudes revealed that they feel the greatest pressure from the media to be thin, followed by their peers and their family. Pressure comes from other sources as well. At the same time elementary-age girls are enchanted by petite figure skaters and pixie gymnasts, they are playing with Barbie dolls, who, if human-sized, would have an eye-popping thirty-nine inch bust and tiny eighteen-inch waist.

If your teens watch TV in the afternoon, they will hear *Oprah Winfrey Show* guests gush to the charismatic Oprah about "how good you look." After she's lost another twenty pounds.

Elsewhere on the small screen, 70 percent of television charac-
ters are thin, according to a survey that found only 5 percent
were overweight. Example: TV's number-one walking billboard
for flesh and bones is Calista Flockhart of Fox's *Ally McBeal*, who
has shrunk from a size 2 to an unbelievable size 0 in the last couple of years. Are young women turned off by her Biafran-like
frame, which can't weigh more than ninety pounds? No, because
young women say that it's better to be too thin than too fat.

A boyfriend can place incredible pressure on a young
woman. If she gains ten pounds, he'll say, "Well, don't get bigger than that." What's she supposed to think a week later when
the scales announce more poundage? What's she supposed to
think when she overhears what guys say about other girls—
"She's porky," or "Look at those thunder thighs"? This is what
she's thinking: *If he says that about her, he'll say it about me.*

If you were to walk into a room of girls, I'd guarantee you
could read these thoughts in many of their minds: "Look at
her. Her legs are so much longer and thinner than mine."
"Look at her figure. She looks like Courteney Cox." "She has
no pimples. How come I'm always breaking out?" "Her hips
are perfect. Mine are so huge." "I wish I were thin."

Thinness has not only come to represent attractiveness, but
success, self-control, and higher economic status as well. The
following are the Thin Commandments, as written by Carolyn
Costin, the clinical director of a California eating disorder
clinic and author of two books.

The Thin Commandments

1. If you aren't thin, you aren't attractive.

2. Being thin is more important than being healthy.

3. You must buy clothes, cut your hair, take laxatives, starve yourself, or do anything to make yourself look thinner.

4. Thou shall not eat without feeling guilty.

5. Thou shall not eat fattening food without punishing yourself afterwards.

6. Thou shall count calories and restrict intake accordingly.

7. What the scale says is the most important thing.

8. Losing weight is good. Gaining weight is bad.

9. You can never be too thin.

10. Being thin and not eating are signs of true willpower and success.

What You Can Do

Since you could go hungry waiting for the mainstream media to present a balanced view of what girls *really* look like, moms and dads must step up and offer encouragement and a counterpoint. Here are some things you can do:

♦ **Watch for overnight changes when your daughter hits her "growth spurt."** Puberty can do amazing things to the body. A five foot, flat-chested girl weighing 110 pounds in the seventh grade can become a five foot, four inch girl weighing 150 pounds who needs a 34C bra as she enters the eighth grade! Of course, she's wondering what hit her. She's going to worry about her new weight or if someone notices the zit on her face. Help her through this difficult time by telling her stories of what you felt during your growth spurts. Compliment her growing body. If she develops a large bust in middle school or high school, she will hear friends tell her that if she loses weight, her chest size will shrink. She may start starving herself. This is when she needs you the most. Discuss the issue with love. Draw her out. Offer to get professional help on losing weight the *right* way.

◆ **If your teen daughter is watching what she eats, watch what you say.** Dinnertime comments such as "Getting chubby, aren't we?" or "Do you really think your body can afford that chocolate cake?" will not win you a Parent of the Year award.

◆ **Repeat after me:** *If you can't say something nice about your child's weight, don't say anything at all.* Let me amend that to include other people as well. Laughing at portly men or pear-shaped women sends the wrong message and reinforces the vilification of overweight people and the glorification of slenderness.

This is what I have to say to parents. Most of my friends with eating disorders weren't fat at all. They were disgustingly skinny and had been disgustingly skinny their entire lives. They had eating disorders because they wanted to please their parents, maintain their weight, and look good for the family. One of my friends felt like she had to lose weight because her parents made fun of her pudgy sister, saying things like, "Why don't you lose weight?" She wasn't overweight; she was just pudgy. My friend became bulimic because she didn't want that to happen to her.

—*Arianne*, age fifteen

◆ **Don't even joke about it.** Even saying, "So, eating again?" could be enough to start your daughter obsessing about food.

◆ **Don't constantly talk about dieting and losing weight in front of your children.** If you're in the midst of a personal struggle with your weight, resist the temptation to give the family a play-by-play description of lost ounces and gained pounds. If the children see you obsessed with counting fat grams and measuring portions, they will become just like you. Gulping diet pills, laxatives, or diuretics shows a persistent concern with body image. If you are dieting, don't make a big deal about it. Quietly go about your business.

◆ **Even if you're dieting, continue serving three well-balanced meals a day.** Children need food to grow and nutrients to fuel puberty. Your desire to skip meals—coupled with making the children feel guilty for being hungry—doesn't do anyone any good. Continue to cook complete meals and eat with your family. Just give yourself smaller serving sizes.

◆ **Give them the facts.** Fact: The average American woman stands five feet, four inches tall and weighs 130 pounds. Fact: Supermodels stand close to six feet tall and weigh between 100 and 110 pounds. Fact: 65 percent of American women wear a size 12 or larger. Fact: Your body shape is much determined by family genes. Fact: It's natural to add some body fat because women must have a certain level of body fat to bear a baby.

   On the other hand, the facts also show that eating disorders are dangerous and carry long-term health effects.

Up to 10 percent of the girls with *anorexia nervosa* die from the disease. Those who survive are left with shrunken organs, bone mineral loss (which leads to osteoporosis later in life), low blood pressure, damaged reproductive organs, and an irregular heartbeat, which can lead to cardiac arrest. Binge eaters develop gall bladder disease, heart disease, and certain types of cancer. The stomach acids being regurgitated do not help the digestive tract. Nor does throwing up make you skinny. If your daughter eats a salad with lettuce, cheese, bacon, and croutons, the first thing to come up is the food that contains the vitamins—like the lettuce. But the bacon and cheese—the fatty parts—all stay in your stomach, where it continues to be digested.

◆ **If your daughter is bulimic, keep an eye out for telltale signs.** Watch for frequent visits to the bathroom, watery eyes and scraped knuckles from gagging, and playing music in the bathroom to muffle purging sounds.

◆ **Tell your children that they look beautiful—early and often.** Alone in her bedroom, your daughter could be looking into a mirror and saying to herself, "You are fat, you are fat. If you could lose just a little more weight, you would be a much better person." If she is saying to herself, "You are fat," who's going to offer a counterpoint? It has to be you, Mom and Dad. Boost her self-image by reminding her how beautiful God made her. Love her even when she's acting unlovable. Boost your child's self-esteem by continually complimenting her gifts, talents, inner beauty, and character qualities rather than her appearance. Let her know that it is not her "outside" that you love or are proud of, but rather her "inside." Love her unconditionally.

- **Remember that eating disorders are very much about control.** Parents constantly harping on their daughter to "do something" about her weight or vowing to "take control" of the situation are backing their daughter into a corner. Often, anorexic girls feel that they have lost all control of their lives, but the one thing they can still reign over is the amount of food they put into their mouths. When anorexia or bulimia becomes a control issue, it's best to seek professional help.

- **Realize that even if she's losing weight, it's hard for her to stop.** Your daughter is thinking: *If I were skinny and beautiful, I'd be popular.* This thinking creates a never-ending downward spiral that often leads to a crash. That's why 105-pound twigs think they are "fat" and have to lose more. Saying, "We've got to fatten you up" is something you should never state to an anorexic teen. I know you're just trying to help, but that will alienate her more than pull her out of her tailspin.

- **Invite her to talk to you.** The last people an anorexic teen wants to talk to are her parents because of the shame she feels. Take the first step. Express your love for her. Tell her that she's the most important person in the world to you. Say that you are willing to help her with anything.

- **If your daughter has a serious problem with anorexia and bulimia, consider getting help.** The best treatment center I've heard about is the Remuda Ranch Center for Anorexia and Bulimia, an Arizona treatment center for women and adolescent girls suffering from eating disorders. "Treatment is a combination of medical, psychological, and nutritional approaches from a faith-based perspective," said

Ward Keller, chief executive officer and founder of Remuda
Ranch. "Each month we receive 600 first-time calls from
individuals seeking treatment, but we have room for only
fifty new patients." Adolescent girls stay an average of sixty
days. "We focus on both the behavioral issues and teach the
patients how to eat appropriately, as well as deal with the
foundational issues of life that drive the eating disorder,"
said Keller. "The problem is not about food; it's a symbol of
something else happening in their lives." For more information about Remuda Ranch, confidential calls can be made
to (800) 445-1900.

Discussion Starters

Do you have any friends with eating disorders?

What did they tell you about their problems?

Are they anorexic or bulimic?

Do they know that eating disorders are unhealthy?

Do you feel pressure to lose weight?

Have I given you that pressure?

Do you have any friends fixated on foods?

Would you feel comfortable coming to me and talking
about any problems you're having with food?

Could you come talk to me about weight issues?

Little kids don't care about body fat or weight. Why do
you care so much?

Are you being truthful about this issue?

12

Body Art

NBA BASKETBALL PLAYER Dennis Rodman's legacy won't be in basketball but in the way he glorified body piercing and tattoos. Rodman, a six-foot, eight-inch rebounding machine, was more of a celebrity rock star than an NBA performer. He first attracted notice when he dyed his short Afro hair in Candyland colors (blue, red, green, and white), threw his Chicago Bulls jersey into the crowd, hung out with Madonna, and treated coaches, referees, and management like a dog treats a fire hydrant.

I credit—or blame—Rodman for being the first to bring "body art"—tattoos, piercings, and cuttings—into the nation's living rooms nearly ten years ago. When he married model Annie Banks in 1993, who bore him a daughter, Alexis, Rodman celebrated these major milestones with a pair of indelible mementos: two tattoos in honor of his wife and child.

It's too bad that Dennis's marriage lasted only eighty-two days. But, once free from the old lady and the responsibility of raising an infant daughter, Dennis hooked up with the Material Girl (Madonna) for a stretch of casual sex, which he catalogued in a raunchy autobiography entitled *Bad As I Wanna Be*.

Kids lapped it up. With each new hair color, tattoo, or pierced body part, Rodman positioned himself as a celebrity icon. Overnight the media and entertainment industry brought body art—the practice of piercing various cartilage, skin, and orifices, or permanently coloring skin with inks and dyes—into the mainstream. No longer were tattoos the province of the circus's tattooed lady, leather-clad Hell's Angels, or jar-headed Marines. It was during the height of Rodman's popularity several years ago that we began noticing tattoos and body piercings on the teens who came to the House of Hope.

Adolescents have taken this fad several steps further since Rodman's heyday. Teens are adorning themselves with an array of earrings, eyebrow rings, nose rings, nose studs, lip rings, chin studs, labrets (a stud through the lower lip), and tongue studs. Many add tattoos: logos of their favorite bands dyed into their biceps, tribal feathers on their chest, or discreet flowers on lower calves. I'll have more to say about tattoos later in this chapter.

As for body piercings, that practice doesn't end at the neckline. Nipples, belly buttons (ouch!), and genitalia (double ouch!) are also pierced by guys and girls alike. As columnist Dave Barry would say, "I'm not making this up." Dennis Rodman had his scrotum pierced, but most male piercers prefer the "Prince Albert," which is performed by inserting a needle-receiving tube into the urethra. The Prince Albert ring goes into and along the urethra and comes out behind the glans on the underside of the penis. The piercing increases erotic stimulation when the ring moves or rotates through the urethra.

Is this sick stuff, or what?

Piercing is just what it sounds like—the piercing of the body with needles ranging from 2 gauge (a horse needle) to 20 gauge (very thin). The ear is most common for both sexes. Even Michael Jordan's squeaky-clean image wasn't tarnished one iota when he began wearing a diamond stud in his left ear.

Nose piercing is a fast riser in the piercing sweepstakes. Teens like to pierce the nostril and septum—the cartilage between the nostrils. Tongues can be pierced in the center, off-center, or horizontal areas. Piercers have used their imagination to find places surrounding the mouth, such as lips and cheeks.

Sitting still and letting someone shoot a needle through a body part is something I could never do. Yet teen adherents talk about being pierced as a "ritual" where painful sensations are part and parcel of the program. They claim their pain is erotic, but I would beg to differ. It stands to reason that the body's nerves will protest rather loudly when a needle is rammed through a nose, tongue, chin, nipple, belly button, or genitalia. While piercing is perceived as making a sensual area more sensitive, teens can't count on that happening. Earlobes punctured too repeatedly can stop being erogenous. I read that one woman had so many rings through her labia that her genitalia went numb.

Piercing generally falls into two categories. The first type is purely aesthetic and visual. Facial and navel piercings fall into this category. Adherents claim that the second category—

genitals and nipples—provides more sensual delights. In a word, young people are piercing their most sensitive parts because they claim it makes sex better. Piercings do not cut across gender lines; customers are split about 50/50 for males and females. Navel piercings, the most popular presently, take the longest to heal.

Our Rules

We have rules at the House of Hope, as you know, and our rules regarding body piercing are that girls are allowed two earrings in each ear and the guys are not allowed earrings or studs anywhere.

When Carissa arrived at the House of Hope, Dennis Rodman didn't have anything on her. Carissa had pierced her beautiful body *nineteen* times—mainly on her face. She was reluctant to tell us where the nineteenth piercing was located, if you catch my drift.

Her first non-ear piercing came when she was fourteen. Someone had told her to be careful not to sever a nerve that controlled the eye muscles, but Carissa took a safety pin, pinched her right eyebrow, and jabbed the pin through. She worked the pin through skin and muscle, and then removed it to allow a friend to insert a lightweight hoop ring. Then it was on to the left eyebrow.

Over the next few weeks, Carissa became enamored with the half-dozen hoop rings across her eyebrows. She decided to become even *more* adventurous. She paid a body-piercing "artist" at a downtown tattoo parlor to pierce her nose, chin, and tongue, the latter in two places. She removed her facial piercings when she was home with her mother, but once she was out the door, in they went again. Then Carissa wanted a piercing she could hide from her mother, so she pierced her belly button. *Ha, ha, you can't see it.*

When I asked her why she pierced herself so many times, Carissa replied, "Body piercing was a fad for me. All my friends were doing it. You know how the rich kids buy Abercrombie & Fitch? Well, piercing was for the poor folks. All the rich kids could wear their Abercrombie or Banana Republic clothes, but all of us poor kids had our piercings."

"Now, Carissa, help me out here," I said. "I can understand some of the face piercings, but the tongue? Didn't it bother you to have your tongue pierced and two metal studs in your mouth?"

"Actually, they were fun to have," said Carissa, "although I will never wear tongue piercings again. They are used for perversion and yuck stuff."

"Yuck stuff?"

"You know, oral sex. Tongue rings started in the lesbian world twenty years ago. Since then they've become more mainstream. Another thing is that kids know that when they take acid and ecstasy, their jaws will lock so they chew gum, suck on Blow Pops, use a pacifier, or use their tongue rings to take pressure off their teeth. When I used my tongue ring to keep my jaw moving, I would wake up in the morning with a swollen and crusty tongue. That was so disgusting! I had scabs on the inside of my mouth."

If your teens are into piercing, that's a good signal that you've lost control of their upbringing. For all their mainstream trappings, pierced teens are still regarded as being on the fringe elements of society, and I hope it remains that way.

Most likely, you will have to bring in a third party to discuss your teen's piercing. Much repair work will have to be done to your relationship, because piercing is a manifestation that your teen rejects your values and your boundaries.

Unglued and Tattooed

Even worse than piercings are tattoos since, for all intents and purposes, tattoos are forever. Archaeologists even discovered Egyptian mummies with blue tattoo marks!

No one knows when the practice of tattooing began, but the process is relatively simple. A tattoo artist injects colored pigment into small deep holes made in the skin with an electric needle. The tattoo is often extended to include scarification, which consists of skin incisions into which irritants may be rubbed to produce a raised scar.

The Old Testament prohibited the Israelites from the practice, it was forbidden by Mohammed, and a Roman Catholic council condemned tattoos in 787. The Nazis tattooed Jewish prisoners during the Holocaust—and the dwindling number of survivors bear those indelible numbers today. Until the last decade or so, Western cultures regarded tattooing as a somewhat vulgar practice performed in back-alley tattoo "parlors."

Tattoos can be removed, but the methods for tattoo removal are not for the squeamish. Excision—cutting the skin off—involves an injection of a local anesthetic to numb the area, after which the entire tattoo can be surgically removed. A new procedure is laser removal in which pulses of light are directed onto the tattoo breaking up the tattoo pigment. More than one treatment is necessary to remove the tattoo.

Tattoos are everywhere. I got mine at fourteen—a rose on my ankle. It's not like the cheesy rose that everyone gets, but one I designed myself. I didn't want a butterfly, mushroom, or some dragon. I really don't think there is anything wrong with tattoos.

—Lorian, age sixteen

I don't have a tattoo, but I want to get one when I'm older. I love what they express. But I'm going to wait until I'm eighteen to see if I'm still into it.

—Daniel, age sixteen

Now that I've painted a horrible picture of Rodman look-alikes, you're probably wondering, *How can I keep my teens from piercing their skin? How I can I keep them out of the tattoo parlor?*

If you have a rebellious teen used to coming and going as he pleases, it will be very difficult to forbid him to pierce or tattoo his body. You might say something like this about tattoos: "Don't forget that they hurt, they bleed, and they last forever."

Teens, of course, can't imagine themselves as middle-aged or especially as old geezers. What will today's teens look like fifty years from now—their backs, arms, and legs violated by fading tattoos?

Another tack would be to stall your teen. You might say something like, "Ally, this is a decision that must be made when you are out on your own and supporting yourself. If you want a tattoo when you're an adult, that's your choice. For now, I want to protect you from making a life-long decision. Many businesses and companies won't hire tattooed or pierced-up kids."

Remind your teen that fads and "what's new" change very quickly. Dennis Rodman is a has-been, a washed-up basketball player and a B-movie actor. Who cares about him these days? If your teen had replicated Rodman's favorite tattoo on his body, how would he feel now?

Carving Away

Another issue regarding "body art" must be addressed, and that's a practice known as "carving" or "cutting." We are seeing more and more teens arrive at the House of Hope with scars on their legs, arms, and wrists. Teens who get an Exacto knife and take their time slicing their flesh claim a sense of power or a tremendous relief of stress in their lives. It's as though they cut the pain out and brought it to the surface so it could heal.

"Carving is like self-mutilation," said Josh, one of our seventeen-year-olds. "Carving brought me pain that I felt I deserved. I found that the physical pain of taking a razor and digging into my skin overtook the emotional pain that I was experiencing. I couldn't take how badly I was feeling, so I had to express it somehow. I got really creative, too, when I discovered that you can mix salt and ice to create an acid burn. I have a scar on my left hand from the acid."

Some teens are allowing themselves to be branded with heated metal. Thankfully, this is a fringe practice.

If your teen has been practicing self-mutilation, it's a manifestation of something painful inside. Mutilations, carvings, piercings, and tattoos are definite warning signs of poor self-esteem and that your child is becoming unglued. I'm sorry that I don't have any answers beyond that, but you will need to enlist professional help.

Discussion Starters

How popular is body piercing today with your classmates?

Are any of your friends into body piercing?

Have you ever watched someone receive a body piercing?

What was that like? Did it hurt?

Why do you think teens like to pierce their bodies?

If you could pierce something on your body, what would
it be? Why?

How popular are tattoos?

What kind of tattoos are your friends having done?

What do you think those tattoos will look like when
they are Grandfather's age?

Do you know anybody into carving?

Why do you think they do it?

Do you think it's dangerous?

Will the scars stay with them until they die?

13

Just a Click Away

FIVE YEARS AGO, it wasn't necessary to write this chapter, but what you're about to read may save you and your teens from a lifetime of hurt and regret.

The invention of the World Wide Web and a family's easy access to the Internet via a modem and home computer have brought cataclysmic changes in the way pornography and inappropriate material are made available to teenagers. Everything from erotic images to bestiality to "kiddie porn" to hate speech to directions on how to make pipe bombs materializes in seconds as colorized pixel bits.

I am *very* concerned about the Internet and the danger it poses to teenagers because it's rather easy for them to find themselves in some awful porn-related Web sites. It's child's play! Don't believe me? Pretend you are a high school student and you've been given a homework assignment to write a report on Louisa May Alcott's *Little Women*. You begin your research by typing *little women* in a search engine such as HotBot. The browser brings you access to 500,000 "matches." Some of those matches link you to legitimate Web sites referencing Miss Alcott's famous book. But others point you toward sites like the "Little Women Forum," a Web address dedicated to "small breasts, tiny tops, and itty, bitty titties." I kid you not.

Welcome to cyberspace, and it's a brave new world out there. In case you're not computer savvy, you better know that your teens are. What do you think they're learning at school? After all, 89 percent of public schools are connected to the Internet, and students are taught how to navigate the World Wide Web. What makes this interesting—and a matter of grave concern—is that the Internet is built on the back of the porn industry. Did you know that 60 percent of all Web site visits are sexual in nature? Did you know that sex is the number one searched-for topic on the Internet?

For all their popularity, virtual companies such as Amazon.com—the leader in e-commerce—aren't profitable yet. But tens of thousands of hard-core XXX-rated sites are raking in *mucho* bucks to the tune of $1 billion a year. The *Washington Post* has called the Internet the largest pornography store in the history of mankind.

There's a reason why so many deviant men and testosterone-laden teens frequent this cyberstore. In the old days, you had to get in a car or take a bus to the seedy part of town to watch a dirty movie or buy glossy magazines depicting naked bodies performing sexual acts. That's no longer the case. Every kind of pornography imaginable can be brought to your teen's computer screen in the privacy of his bedroom. Sometimes it's free; sometimes he must pay. If it's the latter, all he needs is Dad's credit card—or a friend's. Many sites, however, allow voyeurs to download dirty pictures without paying a cent. They figure a long peek will entice viewers to lay down some serious money—usually $19.95—to see more. Their advisory ("You must be eighteen years old to enter this site") is a joke.

Then there are teen boys who don't *intentionally* seek out Internet porn. They stumble across XXX-rated sites by misspelling a word during a search (boys, toys, etc.), coming upon a "stealth site" (there's a *big* difference between whitehouse.com and whitehouse.gov), or innocently typing in a brand name, which links them to pictures of naked women. Twenty-five percent of porn sites are estimated to use popular brand names. The top ten are: Disney, Barbie, CNN, Honda, Mercedes, Levis, ESPN, NBA, Chevy, and Nintendo.

According to a Yankelovitch Partner survey, 91 percent of children accessing objectionable Web sites did so unintentionally. The same survey found that 62 percent of parents were unaware that their children had accessed objectionable sites.

> It doesn't take long to notice that women are used and abused in pornography. There has never been a pornographic movie or Web site that added dignity or grace to a woman or caused a man to feel that a woman is special and should be treated as such.
>
> —*Karen*, a House of Hope counselor

Dangers Lurk

Why am I concerned about pornography? Because it warps young minds regarding the beauty of sex. Teens hooked on Internet porn sites develop sexual attitudes that are coarse and debased. They want to "act out" what they see on the computer monitor.

For instance, teen boys influenced by porn believe:

1. All women want "it" any time day or night.

2. When a woman says "no," she really means "yes." This so-called rape myth is perpetuated throughout all strata of porn.

3. All women are incredibly built with large bosoms, tiny waists, full thighs, and tight buns. Is this the real world? No.

4. Women enjoy deviant sexual acts. Again, not true.

5. Women's basic role in life is to give sexual pleasure to men.

As for adolescent girls, a vast majority thinks porn is icky, but a few are fascinated with the images. That fascination turns to daydreaming and playing "what-ifs" in their minds. They begin thinking that what is abnormal is really normal.

Are these the attitudes you want your teens to grow up with? I hope not. You want to nip Internet porn in the bud because pornography is progressive and addictive. Believe it or not, pictures of a man and woman having intercourse get old after a while. Guys need something more stimulating, such as pictures of women being tied up and raped or a dominatrix performing S&M. Viewing pornography is addictive and progressive. Men need more and more stimulation, which is why they eventually seek images of women having sex with dogs, couples spreading feces on each other, or scenes of bloody mutilations. I cannot warn you enough about the sick, sick stuff out there.

I'll never forget when convicted mass murderer Ted Bundy was scheduled to be executed in Florida State Prison back in

1989. On the eve of his date with the electric chair, Bundy gave a jailhouse interview to Dr. James Dobson, president of Focus on the Family and a person long involved in the fight against pornography.

Bundy told Dr. Dobson that his journey to where he was at that moment—facing certain execution in a matter of hours—began as a young boy twelve or thirteen years old when he found soft-porn magazines in trash cans near his home. He was fascinated by this pornography, and he wanted more. Bundy graduated to harder, more explicit porn—including "detective novels" that featured violence against women.

The interview, captured on a video called *Fatal Addiction*, featured this exchange between Dr. Dobson and Ted Bundy:

Dr. Dobson: Now I really want to understand this. You had gone as far as you could go in your own fantasy life with printed material. Then there was this urge to take that little step or big step over to a physical event.

Ted Bundy: Right. And it happened in stages, gradually. It didn't necessarily, to me at least, happen overnight. My experience with pornography that dealt on a violent level with sexuality is that once you become addicted to it—and I look at this as kind of an addiction—I would keep looking for more potent, more explicit, more graphic kinds of materials. Until you reach the point where the pornography only goes so far. You reach that jumping-off point where you begin to wonder if maybe actually doing it will give you that [satisfaction] which is beyond just reading about it or looking at it.

Chilling, isn't it? Bundy admitted killing more than twenty women in four states, snuffing the innocent lives of young women and teen girls and absolutely devastating the families they left behind.

More Than Just Porn

I know that there are benefits that make it worthwhile to have the Internet in your home. The Internet can open up educational vistas that were never available before. You can take a virtual tour of Buckingham Palace or explore the art found in the New York Museum of Art. This extraordinary communications vehicle delivers millions of resources to your fingertips.

At the House of Hope, we have found that access to the World Wide Web has provided exciting educational advantages for our teens. They use the Internet to do copious amounts of research that would have taken days in a city library. We monitor their use, however, and we use "blocking" software, about which I'll have more to say later.

My concerns about the Internet, however, stretch beyond casual access to inappropriate content. Daterape.org, which billed itself as a "one-stop shop for all your date rape needs," was finally shut down by its Web hosting company following a volume of complaints. The site offered a $49.99 kit that included a *How to Date Rape Properly* manual, "Shut-the-Hell-Up-Bitch" duct tape, and a medical prescription guide to check the side effects of certain drugs. How thoughtful.

If Web sites aren't pushing the envelope of human decency in the area of rape, then thousands of other Web sites and chat rooms are promoting violence, spewing hate speech toward minorities, and outlining easy-to-follow directions for making pipe bombs.

Chat rooms can be especially dangerous, especially to young women. An MSNBC survey found that women favor chat rooms twice as much as men. Sexual predators have easy and anonymous access to unsuspecting kids they "meet" in chat rooms. They'll strike up a conversation and then ask your daughter to go to "instant messaging" (a form of one-on-one online chat), where they begin developing a cyber relationship. In a chat setting, there's no way to know *anything* about the person with whom you're "talking." Researchers call them "gender switchers" or "posers." Men, it is believed, switch roles online more than women.

Let's say a "gender hacker" posing as a teenage girl asks your daughter to meet him. Don't think it can't happen? The newspapers are filled with stories about a "dirty old man" getting caught in a hotel room with a fourteen-year-old girl that he met in a chat room.

That point was driven home to us when we received a frantic phone call from Hailey's mom, asking us if we could take in her daughter right away. It seems that Hailey had a little secret: some friends she had met in a chat room. One asked her to rendezvous in a nearby motel room, so Hailey ran away for a clandestine meeting. Her mother, naturally concerned about the whereabouts of her daughter, noticed that she had left her pager behind. She asked police to trace the last number that Hailey received, which they traced to the motel.

A police officer knocked on a door, which two men and a woman answered. They tried to run for it because they were making preparations to prostitute Hailey. The young girl ran into her mother's arms and burst into tears.

Hailey was one of the lucky ones, as was a mother named Teresa Strickland, who cried as she testified before a U.S. subcommittee on children and families that a forty-three-year-old man found her teenage daughter through the Internet and

convinced her and a friend to run off with him. The daughter
and her friend escaped from the man, who was sent to prison
for felonies involving child pornography and exploitation.

FBI officials testified at the same hearing that they have
arrested hundreds of suspected child molesters through
undercover monitoring of Internet chat rooms. According to
the National Center for Missing and Exploited Children, a
Web site (cybertiplin.com) created in 1999 to take complaints
about suspicious or illegal Internet activity, has received more
than twenty thousand complaints.

"Cyber sex is the crack cocaine of sexual addiction," said
Dr. Robert Weiss of the Sexual Recovery Institute. Cyber sex
is addictive. If your teen son is spending an inordinate amount
of hours in his room surfing the Internet, he could be among
the twenty-five million Americans who visit cyber sex sites
between one to ten hours per week—usually at home after
school, when working parents are not at home. A survey
released in 2000 demonstrated that at least 200,000 Internet
users are hooked on porn sites, X-rated rooms, or other sexual materials online.

If you think this is just a "guy's problem" because they are
hardwired this way, then know this: while boys prefer visual
erotica twice as much as women, girls favor chat rooms twice
as much as boys. According to *Time* magazine, seventeen million kids ages twelve to eighteen were online in 1998; that figure is expected to grow to forty-two million by 2003.

A good friend, Donna Rice Hughes, made me aware of this
problem. If you're thinking, *Where have I heard that name?* you
have a good memory. Back in 1987, when she was Donna Rice,
this young woman was caught up in the Gary Hart scandal
(Donna was having an affair with the presidential candidate).

After straying from her spiritual roots, Donna recommitted herself to God and her faith. She married and settled down. In the mid-1990s, Donna met Dee Jepsen, president of Enough Is Enough, a nonprofit organization dedicated to addressing the sexual exploitation of children, women, and men by illegal pornography. When Dee told Donna that one of the harms of pornography is the perpetuation of the rape myth—that when a woman says no, she really means yes—Donna realized for the first time that she had been victimized in this manner when she lost her virginity against her will at the age of twenty-two.

Donna asked how she could help. Enough Is Enough needed a spokesperson to increase public awareness on the insidiousness of pornography, and Donna fit that role. She joined the organization as vice president of public relations and quickly emerged as a nationally known advocate for protecting children on the Internet. We've become friends since I served on the national board of Enough is Enough. Donna has given over 1,200 TV and magazine interviews in the last few years on this topic and authored the book *Kids Online: Protecting Your Children in Cyberspace* (Revell). She helped me come up with some advice on how you curb Internet porn and keep your kids safe.

1. Keep the computer in a public area. It's hard to monitor Internet use behind closed doors. Place the family computer in the family room or some other area that is out in the open. That way you can "drop in" unexpectedly. I would be very reluctant to allow a teen unencumbered Internet access in his bedroom.

2. Install blocking software or subscribe to an Internet service provider (ISP) that screens out pornographic sites. Blocking software such as Cyber Patrol, Bess, Bonus.com,

Cybersitter, SurfWatch, and Net Nanny use teams of information specialists, parents, and teachers to assist in classifying content. Please know that filtering solutions are not 100 percent foolproof or perfect, not when hundreds of new porn sites come online each day. Clean ISPs are harder to find, but an Internet search should yield a company or two worth checking out. Donna highly recommends familyclick.com, a filtered Internet service provider that has five access levels.

It will be interesting to see what happens in Australia, where the government banned pornographic Web sites in 2000. Australian ISPs are also required to offer their customers filtering software. Internet content believed to be sexually explicit, overly violent, or otherwise offensive receive an "RC" rating for "refused certification." These offensive sites are ordered to "take down" their offensive pages by the Australian Broadcasting Authority. Rather than comply, the porn sites relocate to a U.S.-based server and are back in business—usually within twenty-four hours.

3. Check your teens' "Bookmarks" or "Favorite Places." Netscape and Internet Explorer allow users to "bookmark" their favorite Web sites. Check their browsers for telltale signs of where they've been spending their time in cyberspace. You can also do a search for .jpg or .gif files to find downloaded pictures.

4. Check your credit card statement. Many parents barely glance at their monthly credit card statements. What about you? See any unexplained charges? Porn companies often call themselves by innocuous names to disguise what they really are.

5. Spend some time online with your teen. You need to get up to speed with the Internet and what this is all about. Ask him to show you around the World Wide Web.

6. Only allow your child to use instant messaging with people you know and approve. You should sit in and monitor your daughter's instant messaging. Watch for inconsistencies in statements. After all, you have more experience in judging people than she. Make sure that she does not have an online profile or give out personal information. Remind her that individuals who ask what you look like are often seeking sex.

7. Don't let your child surf the Net late at night. Just like city streets, weird things happen in the wee hours.

8. Tell your child never to give someone your phone number or street address and never, ever to meet someone in person, unless you are with them. There are modern-day Ted Bundys out there, waiting for prey.

9. Clean up your act. You don't have much credibility raising the Internet porn issue with your teens if you have *Playboy* lying around the coffee table or frequent porn sites yourself. Isn't it time you left this degrading stuff behind? If you need help, consult a counselor or pastor.

10. Finally, don't let Internet use dominate their lives. Teens need to be doing other things than spending six hours a day on the Internet. Limit use and plan things you all can do together to promote fellowship, conversation, and recreation.

Discussion Starters

What is pornography?

Do you think looking at pictures of naked women or
people having sex is wrong? Or do you think it is
a good thing?

How do you feel when you see those images?

Do you think porn degrades women?

Have you ever accidentally stumbled upon a porn Web
site?

Did you explore that sight?

If so, how did that make you feel?

Do you like chat rooms?

Which one is your favorite?

Have you ever met creepy people in the chat rooms?

14

Lots to Talk About

THIS WILL BE A HODGEPODGE CHAPTER, touching on a variety of subjects prevalent in our teens' world.

Home Alone

It's three o'clock in the afternoon. Do you know what your children are doing after school?

They're eating, using the bathroom, and watching television. Lots and lots of television. (That's if they are not entertaining a classmate lover in their bedrooms—see Chapter 9.) The University of Michigan's Institute for Social Research completed a study in 2000 of children who arrive home from school unsupervised. The students filled out journals describing how they spent the first one hundred minutes after arriving home from school. (The survey found that nearly one-fourth of children ages eleven to twelve are home alone; that figure rises as children reach the teen years.)

Only 13 percent of the students made studying their top priority upon crossing the threshold. The rest took their time getting something to eat and flipping on the TV. What are they watching? Mindless soap operas, raunchy talk shows such as Jerry Springer and Rikki Lake, suggestive music videos on MTV, and uncut movies from premium channels such as HBO and Showtime.

MTV seems to be the biggest draw for teens. Several MTV shows, which come on different times during the day and evening, are *very* popular these days. If you think that MTV is just an endless loop of music videos, then you're mistaken. My House of Hope kids said they were hooked on MTV-produced programs such as *Road Rules*, *Real World*, and *Loveline*.

Road Rules is about a half-dozen "cast members"—strangers selected by MTV—who share a recreational vehicle and embark on a series of missions, or "face-offs." The motley group abandons all money and credit cards at the beginning of each journey, but they can earn money for food, and other expenses by completing their missions. Cast members are sent on a variety of adrenaline-surging activities: a frozen waterfall in Colorado, skiing the slopes of British Columbia, hang gliding over a "cloud forest" in Costa Rica, and swimming among the dolphins and sea lions in Baja California's warm waters. A camera crew follows them 24/7, catching every moment for the kids at home.

Real World is about seven young people from different countries living together in one house. Some pair up, including gay and lesbian couples. *Loveline* is a live, question and answer session regarding teen sex. Lots of talk about erections and oral sex.

Real World would sometimes be broadcast all day on the weekends, and that's all I wanted to do—just watch that show hour after hour. I never wanted to do stuff with my mom. The show was big on showing lesbian couples as normal.

—*Karen*, age fifteen

Parents, you need to have some rules regarding TV viewing. First, I would limit the TV to no more than one hour *after* all homework is done and *after* dinnertime. There's no reason why the TV has to be on nearly eight hours a day, which is the national average. But how can you keep the TV turned off when you're not home? There are newer TVs that can be programmed to come on or show certain channels only after a password has been tapped into the remote control. That should limit TV viewing. But what if your teen just has to watch her favorite show, which comes on at four o'clock? You can tape the show for later viewing. Let technology work for you.

Our TV policy at the House of Hope is that the teens can watch sporting events, historical documentaries (like those found on the History Channel), or a handful of prime time shows that meet our standard, such as *Touched by an Angel* and *Seventh Heaven*. Our goal is to try to get the kids to use their minds constructively, which means we promote reading instead of being couch potatoes. Actually, we keep the House of Hope teens so busy that they get out of the habit of watching TV. You can set the same ground rules in your household as well. It can be done!

Teen Reasoning

The subject was teens and parents, and Tyler was waxing eloquent in an interview for this book.

"If you tell kids they can't do something, they'll go off and do it anyway. But if you tell them why it's not good, then they'll learn why."

I nodded, my body language urging him to continue.

"But if you tell someone not to go out and kill himself, and he goes off and kills himself anyway, he won't learn from it."

No, Tyler, I guess a teen who commits suicide won't learn from it.

That's what I love about teens. They constantly amaze you with their insights, their energy, and their ability to make off-the-wall remarks.

The next time your teen utters something that doesn't make sense, forgets a doctor's appointment, or paints his face in school colors for the big homecoming football game, realize that he's still a construction zone.

If it's any consolation, scientists think they are making progress in understanding why teenagers act so much like...teenagers. Neuroscientists led by Elizabeth Stowell of UCLA's Lab of Neuro Imaging used magnetic resonance imaging (MRI) to compare the brains of twelve-to-sixteen-year-olds to those of people in their twenties.

The researchers unexpectedly found that the frontal lobes underwent the greatest change between puberty and young adulthood. What's the significance of this discovery? The frontal lobe of the brain is essential for inhibiting impulses, regulating emotions, exercising self-control, organizing, and planning—attributes that we associate with mature young people.

So the next time your teens say something that doesn't make sense, know that scientific evidence supports their short-circuited critical thinking!

Gay and Lesbian Issues

Back in my day, homosexuality was known as the "love that dare not speaketh its name." Times have changed, and today it's no big deal for gays and lesbians to come out of the closet. In the beginning, they made a plea for tolerance. Now homosexuals are asking for acceptance—even gay marriage, which is why rational people on both sides of this issue say that we are in the midst of a cultural war of values regarding the subject.

We have had kids at the House of Hope who are gay, bisexual, or confused about their sexual identity. It doesn't matter. We love them right where they are, and they know we do.

> I've met tons of lesbians in the club scene, and tons of girls who were bi. Many of them told me they wanted to try it out and see how it works. I think ecstasy, which has lots of seductiveness tied into it, is one reason why teens experiment. Kids on ecstasy touch and massage each other because their muscles become tense from the drugs. In your head, you're thinking, "This is not really okay," but you go ahead. And then your girlfriend starts kissing you, and things just go from there.
>
> —*Kristin*, age seventeen

> Girls can walk around and hold each other's hands, but they're only friends. Guys can't do that since they would be looked upon as "queers." I'm probably one of the most sensitive guys at the House of Hope because I cry a great deal, and I like hugs. But that doesn't mean I'm attracted to guys.
>
> —*Jeremy*, age seventeen

Sometimes we feel like the House of Hope is on the cutting edge of where the culture is headed. In the alternative lifestyle arena, we've noticed in the last five years more girl-girl pairing off. These girls are looking for attention and intimacy because they were not getting it from their fathers back home. It's important for girls to have warm relationships with their fathers because a dad can affirm his daughter's femininity and give her a feeling that "it's okay to be a woman."

Another reason why young girls are attracted to the lesbian lifestyle is because they were molested by older men or family members in their early years of adolescence. Who wouldn't be turned off or sickened by heterosexual sex under such cruel circumstances?

Teens attracted to homosexuality can be helped, but counseling will be needed. Our House of Hope counselors spend hours digging deeper and deeper into this issue, and we have had some notable successes. But the gay teen has to want to make a lifestyle change before we can help.

Running Away

Although it's not as prevalent as some of the teen problems discussed earlier in this book, running away occurs often enough that I feel I must address this issue. I would estimate that more than three-fourths of the House of Hope teens have run away at least once during their adolescence. They leave home for a variety of reasons: parents don't care, parents care too much, they want to see the world, or some friend urged them on.

We can't stop teens from running away from the House of Hope, although we try to talk them out of it. Some are just determined to run. Just ask April. She ran away *twelve* times.

"Every time I ran away, I came back high on drugs," said April. "My counselor would ask me whether I did drugs while I was away, and I would say no. My eyes were bloodshot, I was really hungry, and I was just sitting there like an idiot, so she had to know I was all messed up on drugs. Running away was crazy. It was so dumb."

Each time April ran away, she would return two or three days later. She didn't want to come back, but she didn't want to stay out on the streets, either.

"What made you decide not to run away anymore?" I asked April.

"I began seeing what I was doing with my life," replied April. "I realized that if I kept running away, I would be put in jail."

"If I were your parent, what could I do to keep you from running away?" I asked.

"Not much. If you're strict and told me not to run away, that would make me want to run all the more. I think you should tell me what the consequences are. Talk about the dangers on the streets, how predators are lurking around."

"Do kids listen?" I probed.

"It depends on how stubborn they are. It took me about six years before I stopped running."

"How common is running away with teens these days?"

"It's very common."

"Where did you usually stay or sleep?"

"I could usually go to someone's house and stay with her for a couple of days. It's kind of like barhopping."

"How about money to eat?"

"That's a tough one. If you don't have a good 'hook-up,' someone who can feed you and house you, then you usually end up in prostitution or selling drugs," said April.

"How long does a runaway stay out on the streets before coming home?" I asked.

"It depends on if his parents are actually looking for him," she replied. "My dad looked for me constantly until he found me. But if parents don't care and stop bothering to find you, kids can be out on the streets for years."

Kelly told me that she ran away because her mother was never home. "She's a big executive who wasn't easy to live with," said Kelly. "I really wanted Mom to love me and spend time with me. That didn't happen. When she was home, I couldn't do whatever I wanted to do, so I ran."

We have no gates, no fenced areas at the House of Hope. We've had teens announce they are leaving, and out the door they go. We watch them walk down 30th Street. Then we wait for them to return, which they all invariably do since they are cold, hungry, or thirsty, or they don't have any money to buy drugs. They understand before they run that they will be punished by being dropped to Phase I and made to do extra chores. But they come back anyway because they know that we will hug them and continue to love them.

That's the feeling you want to get across to your teens. If you have a strong suspicion that one of them wants to run away (based on his yelling, "Don't tell me what to do or I'll run away!"), give him the option of staying with another family, a place where he could cool off until the storm passes. This could be a good alternative.

The Effects of Film

When the blockbuster movie *Titanic* was released in 1997, nearly everyone wanted to see the movie about the doomed luxury liner because it was such a compelling human drama.

For discerning parents of young teens, however, the PG-13 rating for *Titanic* should have sounded warning bells in your household.

A PG-13 film can mean everything from a "clean" movie dealing with an adult theme (such as the Holocaust) to ninety minutes of nonstop double entendres, chainsaw violence, and sexual mischief. What concerns me is that millions of moms and dads are not thinking critically when it comes to how films are rated by Hollywood. They think that since a film is rated PG-13, the movie must be okay for children thirteen and up. So they drop off their kids at the local cinema with practically no knowledge of what the latest "gotta-see" release is all about.

Another thing happens when you drop your children off at the cinema. You have very little control of what film they may actually see. Once they buy a ticket, they can walk into any of the theatres where R-rated movies are being shown. Instead of watching the latest teen-targeted comedy as planned, they sneak into a *Scream*-like horror flick, rated R for grisly violence. Realistic scenes of decapitation and bloody gore can give them nightmares for weeks.

More and more R-rated movies are being produced these days, although Hollywood makes more money on its PG films. Ted Baehr, who publishes a movie review newsletter called *MovieGuide*, says that Hollywood has been targeting the "Baby Boomlet" children—the 77 million born between 1979 and 1989—for years. In the late eighties and early nineties, Hollywood filmmakers released *The Little Mermaid* and *The Lion King*, but as these boomlet kids entered the teen years (where your kids are), Hollywood stepped up its output of films along the lines of *American Pie*, *Freddy Got Fingered*, and *Scream III*.

MovieGuide, a thirty-two-page publication published every two weeks, offers detailed reviews and thoughtful articles, commentaries, and news about Hollywood. Each review includes a sidebar identifying objectionable content and tries to teach parents and teens how to develop media literacy. "We point out what the film is about, but we try not to say whether to go or not," said Baehr. Call (800) 899-6684 to order a year's subscription, twenty-six issues, for $40.

Another tough thing to do is rent a decent video that the whole family can enjoy. Like books, you really can't tell a video by its cover or the brief synopsis written on the jacket. To find a good video (or an acceptable first-run movie), you can listen to word of mouth. What do friends who hold the same values as you say? You can consult resources such as *MovieGuide*. You can rent a movie from the "Classics" or "Musicals" sections. This might be a good time to have them watch excellent and culturally important movies such as *Gone with the Wind* and *Casablanca*.

In the end, you—the parent—will have to "learn to discern."

Discussion Starters

For kids home alone after school:

Be honest. What's your usual routine for the first hour
   after you arrive home from school?
What would it mean to you if I took a pay cut and
   worked less so I could be home after school?
Do you watch any MTV shows? Are they appropriate?
Is the TV on too much in our household?
What are some of the best shows on TV?
What are some of the worst?

For the topic of homosexuality:

Do you think gays and lesbians are born that way?
Do you know any gay teens at school?
What are they like?
Did you know that there are ex-gays?

For the topic of running away:

Have you ever thought about running away?
Where would you run? Whom would you stay with?
Is running away a common thing today?
Why do kids run away?

For the topic of Hollywood movies:

What's the title of your favorite movie?
What made that movie so good?
What's the worst movie you've ever seen?
What's the grossest movie you've ever seen?
Do scary movies give you nightmares?
How do you feel about R-rated movies? Should teens
    under seventeen be able to see them?

15

Where the Real Hope Is

PERHAPS YOU'VE HEARD of the Peter Lowe Success Seminars—those daylong "yes-fests" that feature live appearances from notables such as George and Barbara Bush, Margaret Thatcher, Colin Powell, Larry King, Joe Montana, and probably the most popular motivational speaker alive today—Zig Ziglar. The Peter Lowe Success Seminars are very successful events, selling out 16,000-seat arenas from coast to coast.

Peter, who lives in nearby Tampa, is a good friend of mine, and he has attended our annual "Humanitarian of the Year" gala dinners in the past. Once when the Success Seminar was in Orlando, Peter invited me and twenty-five girls from the House of Hope to meet backstage with former first lady Barbara Bush. What a special treat that was!

Anyway, Peter always speaks in the middle of the afternoon at the Success Seminars. His topic: the Five Levels of Success. When he comes to the fifth point of his presentation, Peter states that the last level of success is based on God, "who says that all things are possible for those who believe."

That statement certainly captures the audience's attention. Peter continues: "For all intents and purposes, my presentation is over, but if you would like to remain for my fourteen-minute 'bonus session' and learn more about how God fits into this last level of success, please remain in your seats. We will take a one-minute break before we start again."

In a similar fashion, I shall issue the same invitation to stick around, because for all intents and purposes, *Unglued & Tattooed* is over. If you continue to read this chapter, however, I think you will gain a better understanding of what *really* changes teens' lives, and that is believing in a Higher Power called God.

You see, back in the days when I worked at the Orange County Juvenile Detention Center, I knew more *could* be done to help those troubled teens. As I contemplated the situation, I realized that these troubled teens needed a spiritual component in their lives. I had been raised in a loving home where God was a natural and important part of everyday life. We said grace at meals and my parents made the rounds each night, reading Bible stories to my three brothers and two sisters and me before the lights went out.

I thought of those kids at the Orange County Juvenile Detention Center hearing "Lights out" and having no one to comfort them, no one to tuck them in, no one to give them a hug, and no one to remind them that God loves them. (Many troubled teens are driven by self-hate, thinking they are so bad that *nobody* could love them.)

In the public sector, we were not allowed to proselytize or share our faith. I understand the rationale behind these rules, but nonetheless, I knew that unless I could give troubled teens a reason to be good once they left the Orange County Juvenile Detention Center, I could count on one hand the days until they would be wearing orange garb again. That's what spurred me to start the House of Hope as a faith-based home for troubled teens.

Downward Spiral

When teens arrive at our campus, they have reached rock bottom. Many of them know that the House of Hope *is* their last hope because they've bounced in and out of Juvenile Hall and a handful of government-run, taxpayer-funded teen programs. Other teens who come to us have lived a life resembling a living hell, such as Sandi:

> When I was really young, I put newspapers in my pants so her spankings wouldn't hurt so much. As I grew older, my mom slapped me around a lot. It was like she was a rageaholic. She never said, "Bend over the chair, honey, I'm going to spank you." No, it was *boom*, a smack out of nowhere. *Where did that come from?*
>
> One time I yelled back at her when I was ironing my clothes. She grabbed the iron and put it on the back of my hand real quick. That hurt so bad! When I asked her why she did that, she backhanded me and said, "Don't you ever talk back again!" When she got mad, she would take me by my hair and throw me against the wall. Another time I balled my hands into fists to fight back, she grabbed my fists, threw me to the ground, and kneed me in the throat. "If you ever raise a hand at me again, I'll kill you!" she screamed.
>
> —*Sandi*, age fifteen

Sandi needed help, and her mother needed counseling and therapy as well. It all begins when the child is brought to our Orlando campus. Please know that this is not Ward and June Cleaver dropping off the Beaver for a couple of months because he was caught sniffing glue with Lumpy Rutherford. We are talking about seriously dysfunctional families.

When our telephone rings, Brenda answers the call, only to hear a frantic parent (the mother 90 percent of the time) saying, "My teenager is out of control! I don't know what to do. Can you help me?"

"Yes, but first, I need to ask you a few..."

"You don't understand! I need help now! I have to drop off Lori tonight! She's out of control!"

"Calm down, Mrs. Turner," says Brenda.

"It's Alice Scott Turner. I never married."

"Yes, Ms. Turner. Before we can proceed, I have to take a few moments to explain that you just don't drop off Lori and come back for her when she's all fixed. We work with the entire family, and that includes you. May I ask you a few questions?"

With that, Brenda does an initial interview to determine if Lori's father is still in the picture, if the two of them live within a reasonable driving distance of the House of Hope, Lori's date of birth, her status in school, her arrest record, any medication she's on, if she's sexually active, what drugs she has been using, and if there has been any sexual abuse in the home. I can't tell you the number of stepfathers who have sexually abused their innocent teen for a few moments of pleasure.

When Lori is enrolled, her mother signs a legal document giving us custody and control of her child. We are provided with her birth certificate, Social Security number, medical history, and any other pertinent information. Included in that agreement is a provision stating that the parent, or both parents, will attend parenting classes every Tuesday night—two hour classes that teach them how to be a good mother and father. They must also attend a one-hour counseling session each week and visit their child from 3 to 5 P.M. on Sunday afternoons. (We've found that the young people have always wanted their parents to be there for them. This is their chance.) The parents must commit to these appointments; otherwise, the child will have to leave the program. This has happened on rare occasions, meaning that we have delivered some tough love along the way. The parents soon learn that we're serious about the strong guidelines they have to follow.

With that as background, let's pretend that you and your daughter, Brittany, are sitting in my office. We have accepted Brittany into the program, and you have signed all the necessary paperwork. At this point, I usually say something like this:

Brittany, you will find that the House of Hope is a home where love abounds. We are not here by accident. We believe that you have been handpicked and specially selected to stay with us. Nonetheless, I understand that you are unhappy with the way your life has been going. We believe that God has called us to share His love with you— a love that is patient and kind, a love that will cause you to desire change, a love that will heal your deepest hurts.

You will be involved in individual counseling, group counseling and classes, family counseling, Bible studies, work duties, recreation, and an individualized Christian education program that will help you to catch up academically. Your days will be full, but you will grow and learn as never before. Let me remind you that you will also have a lot of fun at the House of Hope. You will live in a house with a loving home environment. Our house staff is committed to helping you, loving you, and, yes, even disciplining you. They will help you learn the skills you need to become a mature young person.

By now, Brittany, you know the House of Hope is a faith-based institution that receives no government money. That gives us the freedom to share with you the opportunity you have to discover a meaningful, exciting, and lasting relationship with Jesus Christ. We will not force Christianity down your throat because that is not the way God wants us to come to Him. Our purpose is to help you develop into the person God created you to be. Psalm 139:13–15 says, "For you created my innermost being; you knit me together in my mother's womb. I praise you because I am fearfully and wonderfully made; your works are wonderful, I know that full well. My frame was not hidden from you when I was made in the secret place. When I was woven together in the depths of the earth, your eyes saw my unformed body. All the days ordained for me were written in your book before one of them came to be." There's another Scripture in the Bible in Malachi 4:6 that says God wants to turn the hearts of the fathers and mothers to their children and the hearts of the children to their parents. That's our sincere prayer for you and your parents.

Welcome to the House of Hope, Brittany. Never forget how special you are to us!

Tucking Them In

We make our teens feel special by loving them as much as we can. One of the ways we love them is by tucking them in every night.

Wait a minute, Sara. Did you say tucking in teenage boys and girls? Aren't they a little old for that?

No, they aren't too old. The practice of tucking in your teens every night is something that you can adopt in your household. Remember when you tucked your preschoolers into bed with a kiss, a hug, and a tug of the bed comforter? But you stopped as they grew older for some reason. Our house parents tuck in every teen every night, not with a kiss as most parents do, but with a warm hug. Yes, our street-hardened boys, some standing six feet, four inches tall and weighing 250 pounds, are "tucked in" at bedtime. Initially, they are not used to this display of love, but after a month or two, they can't go to sleep without the touch of a warm hug and someone praying for them before they fall asleep.

Our tucking-in time is a vital part of "loving them where they are." Frequently, my house staff will report major break-throughs at those times when the teens allow them to show that they really do care about them. One of our counselors, Randy, has filled in at times as a house staff member. When I mentioned to him our standard practice of tucking in the boys before they fell asleep, he thought I was joking. He could understand tucking in little kids or even girls, but hormone-charged teen males with deepening voices and stubble growing on their faces? Here's what happened:

> I come from a hard-core clinical background. When I thought of tucking them in at night, I said to myself, *What is that?* But I decided to give it a try. I went into the boys' bedroom and said, "Okay, guys, it's time for bed." I prayed with them, then I went to each bunk bed and gave the boys a hug, saying, "I really

want to let you know that I love you. See you in the morning."

The looks on their faces said, *Wow, Mr. Randy is tucking us in. That's really weird.* That's because they just know me as one of their counselors. But that evening did something special for the boys and me that's hard to describe, probably because I never had hugs as a child. Later that night, I cried like a baby as I realized that I gave those boys something I had never received. Over the next few days, I couldn't believe the changes in myself. It shook my thinking about a new way to get through to these kids, which was hugs.

I know what Randy is talking about. I'll never forget the time when Josh Carter, the second boy to graduate from the House of Hope, stood up at his graduation and cried his eyes out when he began telling how the "tucking in" affected his life. "I felt so loved by that, and I had done nothing to deserve that love," he bawled. That's why our slogan at the House of Hope is: "The streets and institutions don't tuck them in at night, but we do at House of Hope."

Preparing Them for Their Destiny

We respond in love to these teens at the House of Hope. We don't bash them, we don't scream at them, and we don't tell them that they're bad kids. We pray with them, love them through their problems, and remind them that we all fail. We discipline them when they break the rules, but they expect to be held accountable. We even tell real-life experiences of how we blew it. We help them find their true identity and help prepare them for their destiny.

One of my favorite stories of a changed life involves a young man still with us—Adam. At age seventeen, Adam casts a shadow wherever he goes. He's a big, rawboned kid who stands six foot, one inch tall and weighs 240 pounds. If the House of Hope had a football team, he could be a one-man wrecking crew, a rangy fullback who could run over anybody, which is an appropriate metaphor since Adam was running from a painful past when he came to the House of Hope.

Adam's story begins in South Carolina as a five-year-old boy living in a home with his mother and stepfather. He never knew his real dad, but his stepfather was an unbelievably mean human being. When he wasn't grabbing Adam's mother by the wrists and throwing her on their bed and against the wall, he was slapping and punching her. That physical abuse soon landed on young Adam. An innocent question—"Can I go outside to play?" or "Can I have some cereal?"—was met by a thwack to the head or a kick to the shins.

The abuse took a bizarre turn when Adam was still in kindergarten. One day, while his mother was gone, his step-father brought out an armful of *Hustler* magazines to the living room. It was show-and-tell time: Adam was the student, and his stepfather was the teacher.

The anatomy lessons continued for several years. When he was seven years old, his stepfather made Adam take off his clothes and told him to "hump a pillow" to simulate sexual intercourse. His stepfather never removed his clothes and never touched Adam, but he obviously got his pleasure watching a naked second grader. Naturally, he made Adam promise not to say anything to his mother. Adam was sure he would be killed if he ever did, so he kept his mouth shut. Still, the parental abuse continued. Whenever Adam had friends over, his stepfather would go to his bedroom, leave the door wide open, and masturbate in front of the kids.

All this sexual "acting out" created a desire to try some things. Adam attempted to have sex with his best friend's sister when they were both eight years old. She was willing, but Adam could not do anything to her. Adam's mother knew things were getting really bad when ten-year-old Adam pulled a knife on his stepfather and began screaming at him, all in a desperate attempt to protect his mother. She decided to escape and leave South Carolina and go to her sister's house in Lakeland, Florida. They departed in their dilapidated car with their worldly belongings in four cardboard boxes.

His mom found an apartment and began working full time. Meanwhile, Adam began attending school, but he never had many friends on the playground. He started smoking cigarettes at age eleven to act cool and meet other kids. Within a year, Adam was smoking marijuana regularly and snorting cocaine with seventeen-year-old boys, who took him under their wings. They were involved with a white gang called Folks, which included a few black kids and Puerto Ricans in their ranks. Adam never saw his hard-working mom. His afternoons were filled with smoking cigarettes, getting high, and—now that he had matured—having sex with older girls down the street.

To pay for his drug habit, Adam broke into cars and stole CD players, sunglasses, tapes—anything that he could fence at pawnshops. One time he found a four-pound bag of marijuana in a car with a street value of several thousand dollars. Adam branched out by selling drugs on school campuses. He enjoyed ripping people off by mixing marijuana with oregano or "cutting" cocaine with baking soda. No kids were in a hurry to challenge Adam, who, at age fifteen, topped six feet and two hundred pounds.

Adam operated his little business with the following dictum: *If you don't pay up or mess with me, then I mess with you.* His deadbeat customers received one and only one warning: "Give me my money, or I'll really hurt you." Adam beat dozens of kids to a pulp, and he even walked into homes and pummeled fathers in front of their kids. "I had to let them know who was boss," said Adam. By age sixteen, Adam was out of control; even his mother could see that. A friend of hers told her about the House of Hope, but we were full at the time. We agreed to counsel Adam, however, on an outpatient basis.

The first counseling session with Kevin didn't go so well.

Kevin tried to get his attention. "You will die or end up in jail if you don't listen," he said.

"I don't care," replied Adam, his arms crossed. "I'll do what I want."

"It only works for a little while, but once you fall, you're going to fall really hard."

"I still don't care," Adam replied defiantly. "You can't stop me, nobody can stop me, and I'll do what I want. Just you wait and see."

This type of "dialogue" went on for nine months until we finally had an opening for Adam. Being forced to live at a home for troubled teens—a *Christian* home for troubled teens—ticked Adam off. Suddenly he was around people he didn't like for twenty-four hours a day, around kids who didn't do drugs, didn't steal, and weren't in a gang. What did he have in common with them? As with everyone who comes to the House of Hope, Adam was given chores—cleaning up the kitchen after breakfast, vacuuming the bedrooms, cleaning toilets, and mowing the lawns. Except that Adam didn't know how to do chores, and he had to be shown how to complete the simplest one.

All along, Adam heard about God from our loving staff and from his roommates. He memorized Bible verses, which was part of his go-at-your-own pace education program. He attended our chapel services. It wasn't until nine months later when Adam attended Camp Rain, a summer camp we take the teens to, that he decided to make his peace with God. I'll let Adam finish his story:

> I heard a guy at Camp Rain speak one night, and he asked me if I wanted to change my life, and I had to admit, I really did. I thought about how I should have been dead—like the time a drug dealer put a gun to my head and threatened to blow it off. Now I was being given a chance to change my life all over again. When I grabbed hold of that chance, I felt like a new person. I felt like I had worth, like I had a purpose in my life. It was really cool that God could take an old street dog and turn me into a mighty man.
>
> I still have issues to work on and I still mess up, but now I know who to go to, to ask forgiveness. Everything is going better. More doors are being opened too, and I can't wait to find out what kind of life is waiting for me. I messed up really bad in school, so it may take me a while to get my education and get on to college, but I'm all right with that.

So there you have it—Adam's remarkable story. Remember how, early in this book, you heard about our 95 percent success rate in reuniting teens with their families and getting lives turned around? People ask us what our secret is, and by now I think you know what I'm going to say: It's God changing lives, not the House of Hope. There is no better feeling in the world than knowing that you are loved unconditionally, no matter how good or bad you are, no matter how rebellious or "off the deep end" you are. God will be as big in your life as you will allow Him to be.

And that's the gospel truth.

Who Pays?

People often ask us, "Who pays for kids to come to the House of Hope?" It's certainly not the parents who are knocking on our doors or calling in desperation, since most have spent all their money on unsuccessful secular programs—as many as seven other programs. These parents, however, can afford to pay only 11 percent of our operating costs, which means the 89 percent shortfall must be made up through generous donations of money, time, labor, and food from the Orlando community.

We never turn away anyone who doesn't have the money. In fact, if parents had to pay the whole amount of the actual costs, we wouldn't have been able to help one girl or boy in the House of Hope's fifteen years of existence. Our boys and girls come from every socioeconomic level, but no matter how poor the family is, we ask that they pay something. This restores their pride and makes them feel part of the House of Hope. I remember when Tammy came. Her mother had died, and her father could no longer control her. Tammy slept with every boy she met, and she thought nothing about letting others use her body. Tammy's father had a low-paying job—night watchman, I believe—but every Friday morning at 10 A.M. he arrived to give us a $10 bill. That's all he could afford, and I respected that.

Epilogue

IN CLOSING, I'D LIKE TO SHARE ONE LAST STORY that contains the essence of what parenting through the teen years is all about.

One of my dearest friends—someone who's been with the House of Hope since day one—is Sandy. This remarkable, giving person has an inspirational story to tell, and it begins when she was in her late twenties. At that time, Sandy was struggling mightily to raise three elementary-age children. I say struggling mightily because Sandy had grown up in a broken home—her parents had divorced when she was thirteen years old. That, along with other abuse heaped upon Sandy, crippled her emotionally and shaped her into an extremely fearful person. She had watched her mother abuse alcohol to deaden her pain.

After marrying, Sandy's emotional wounds surfaced whenever she and her husband were invited out with friends.

Because social events made her feel uncomfortable, Sandy found that having a couple of drinks before she left the house took the edge off her apprehension, which eventually caused a drinking problem. On top of that, her husband's adulterous relationships led to a marital breakup and divorce. At age thirty, Sandy was a single parent with three daughters nine and under.

Several years later, I met Sandy at a garage sale. She had pulled her life together with God's help and defeated her alcohol problem. She began talking, and I eagerly listened. We became good friends after that chance meeting. One time, Sandy poured out her struggles, telling me about the tough time she was having parenting three teenagers. When she asked me for advice, I replied, "Sandy, you need to pull in the discipline reins. I believe your girls have too much freedom."

"Easy for you to say!" Sandy said, her face turning red.

Shortly after that, I had a feeling her two youngest daughters had gone to the movies to meet some boys, so I mentioned it to Sandy.

"How could you think such a thing?" Sandy demanded with anger rising in her throat. "My daughters would never do something like that without my permission. Let's go to the movies right now and I'll prove it!"

When we walked into the local movie theater, her two daughters were sitting with two boys. She ordered her two daughters to leave immediately. Sandy cried all the way home.

Sandy realized that she had to lay down ground rules and back up those rules with some disciplinary measures, such as lost privileges. But listen to what Sandy said to her teens: "Now that you understand the consequences of breaking the rules, I will be there for you when you're grounded. In other words, when you're grounded, I'm grounded as well." This meant when her children were confined to the house on Friday or Saturday nights, she baked cookies with her teens, watched a video, brought out a puzzle, or just talked while eating chips and drinking Cokes. Grounding turned out to be a fun, productive bonding time for all of them.

One evening, Sandy's middle daughter, Karry, came home late. Sandy, worried about her daughter's safety, yelled at her. Karry shut down in the face of the verbal onslaught and trundled off to bed. Sandy knew she had gone too far. She stepped into her bedroom and prayed that God would give her guidance. As she knelt next to her bed, Sandy had a feeling her daughter was going to run away. She tiptoed over to Karry's room, knocked on the door, and asked to come in. After apologizing for yelling at her, Sandy sat on the bed and stroked her daughter's hair. Then she gently pulled back the covers, which revealed that Karry still had her clothes on.

This time, Sandy didn't blow up or lose her cool. Instead, she drew Karry close, squeezed her tight, and loved her. She decided to tell Karry that she had prayed and asked God for help in that situation. After listening to her mother's story, Karry was convinced that her mom was telling the truth and was doing what any good parent would do. Sandy's simple words gave her the reassurance she needed.

That evening was a turning point in Karry's life, and today she is a happily married young woman with three children. Karry's story is a great reminder that children *do* love their parents and *do* need love. Deep down, teens know they need guidance, boundaries, and leadership. Parents, it's up to us to give it to them.

Remember: *Keep loving your teens.*

Acknowledgments

I WOULD LIKE TO THANK the hundreds of boys, girls, staff members, and volunteers who have contributed to the House of Hope over the years in ways that cannot be counted. My heartfelt appreciation goes to Richard and Jane Chambers, Sandy Carpenter, Phyllis Dwyer, Carol Brown, Lu Hoin, and Betty Wise for being there from the first day. I also want to express my love and thanks to Mark and Betsy McCormack for opening their hearts to this outreach.

Finally, thanks to Mike Yorkey for catching the vision of the House of Hope and his great assistance in writing this book with me. My sister, Jane Chambers, and my niece, Jennifer Prickett, assisted in the valuable editing process.

Index

Want to Learn More About the House of Hope?

IF YOU WOULD LIKE TO CONTACT the House of Hope to learn more about the organization or to attend one of our training seminars on starting a similar program in your hometown, please contact:

Sara Trollinger
House of Hope
P.O. Box 560484
Orlando, FL 32856
tel: (407) 843-8686
fax: (407) 422-3816
e-mail: houseofhopesara@aol.com
Web: www.houseofhope.com